THE

50 75 100

SOLUTION

BUILD BETTER RELATIONSHIPS

BRYAN FALCHUK, CPT BCS

newbodi.espublishing
Boston, Massachusetts, USA

ISBN: 978-0-9985492-4-8

FOR MY WIFE, SHARON

Also by Bryan Falchuk:

Do a Day: How to Live a Better Life Every Day
Available at http://www.doadaybook.com/shop

The Do a Day Podcast
Listen at http://www.doadaypodcast.com

Articles for Inc. Magazine, The Chicago Tribune, LA Times and other publications
Available at http://www.bryanfalchuk.com/media

FORWARD

As a therapist, I work with couples that are blindsided when they realize that others think, feel and believe differently than they do. This leads an empty feeling of not being heard and understood by each other which is a core reason why people become divided. This puts people into a threatened state where they dig in to their own beliefs and miss the opportunity to learn something valuable about each other.

The 50 75 100 Solution confronts this issue head-on, creating a concrete formula from theoretical ideas and provides a plan of action that is easy to understand and, more importantly, it works. Why does Bryan's *50 75 100 Solution* work? It brings our attention to slowing down our response in order to understand the other person instead of quickly reacting.

A common problem that arises between couples I see in my practice is a "gridlocked issue." This is the kind of problem that keeps coming up over and over again leading to fights that rip at the fabric of a relationship.

An example I frequently see come up revolves around money. One person's path to happiness may be saving so they can feel secure together for the future while the other person wants to live in the moment and spend to have experiences together. The interesting thing is they are both using money to achieve a deeper connection with their partner but going about it in opposite directions. It's as if they are both in a boat trying to reach a destination across a lake called "Happiness" but they are rowing in opposite directions causing them to spin in a circle. They become frustrated with each other, feeling threatened and concerned that their partner is actively trying to sabotage their happiness.

These feelings can pervade into every day interactions causing all kinds of chaos. Simply rowing your direction harder will not get the boat across the lake faster, but will instead make you both dizzy. This is when you need put the oars down and make it your mission to discover *why* your partner finds happiness saving while you find happiness spending. The actual reason will be much deeper than you think and have nothing to do with preventing each other from your respective definitions of happiness. Once you understand that your partner finds happiness in savings because they grew up desperately poor and never want to feel that again, you can see your partner's happiness seeking for what it is and not as a roadblock to your happiness seeking. Understanding this unlocks your ability to compromise to create a solution that gets both of you rowing the boat in the same direction to reach your common destination of "Happiness".

The 50 75 100 Solution begins with this notion of Happiness Seeking, which reminds us that other people do not necessarily have intent to hurt us with their actions. They are simply trying to seek their own happiness.

It goes on to teach about how we are all Interconnected, which makes us aware of being a part of a bigger whole as well as gives us the reassurance that we can have influence in a struggling relationship even if the other person does not seem to want to change the situation.

Finally, in learning about Impermanence, we are reminded that situations change and it will not always be this hard so we can handle being in the moment even if it is painful because being present and responding differently may shift the dynamic and create something better.

The 50 75 100 Solution builds on these ideas beautifully and embraces Mahatma Gandhi's challenge to "Be the change that you wish to see in the world." When you are ready to turn a *divided* relationship into a *united* relationship, this book will provide you with a solid plan to do so with success.

A dynamic shift away from a struggling relationship and into one that is full of meaning and happiness is what Bryan's *50 75 100* formula is designed to accomplish and I use it with my clients. My hope is that you will also find the value in bringing these ideas into your life as we all have relationships that could be better for us, for the other person, and for those around us.

– Terah Harrison
Licensed Professional Counselor
Host of *Make More Love Not War*

"Conquer anger with non-anger.
Conquer badness with goodness.
Conquer meanness with generosity.
Conquer dishonesty with truth."

–The Buddha
(from *Dhammapada*, verse 223)

CONTENTS

I. BEFORE THE MATH

I am like you. I have lived a life filled with ups and downs. Through my journey, I have discovered a philosophy which has allowed me to overcome the challenges of life and achieve the things I set my heart and mind to. I call that philosophy "Do a Day", and I shared it with the world in a book of the same name.

Do a Day has been a powerful solution for me in overcoming things like obesity and extreme anxiety while achieving things I never thought possible like running a marathon. It has also been the basis of a rewarding career as an executive in successful businesses and a certified life and executive coach for people I have helped to do deep, introspective self-discovery to unlock their true, enduring motivation. That work has allowed me dig into what makes people tick at the deepest level, and how to help them find that core of their being when they need it most.

From discovering this power within, we point that motivation—our *why*—toward our most inspiring goals that will take real effort and action to achieve. To achieve them, we free ourselves from the judgment of yesterday, while simultaneously letting go of the anxiety we feel for all that lies ahead. That is, we make choices *today*, in support of our goals, without the crushing weight of past mistakes or fear and anticipation of the future.

While *Do a Day* is powerful—it both helped me change my life and is the tool I use to help others change theirs—something that has always remained a struggle for me are relationships. This is because, unlike so many other goals in my life, such as losing weight or achieving career success, I have never seen them as being within my control.

These difficult relationships may be at home, at work, with friends, strangers or really with anyone, anywhere. No matter what I have achieved in my personal transformation journey, I still often encounter situations where real dysfunction and pain with others exist.

These situations can make it difficult to fully achieve the success and positivity we desire. However, just because something is hard does not mean it is impossible.

Through *Do a Day*, I have learned that lesson many times over.

If you achieve great success in one area of your life only to face strife, a lack of support, attacks or any other relationship problem, it can make you feel as if your achievements elsewhere don't matter or at least not enough for your overall life to be a truly happy one.

We do, of course, have a choice as to whether we let someone else's behavior dictate our happiness. If someone argues with you or does not support you, that does not mean you cannot be happy. You can choose the extent of their behavior's impact on you.

What I seek, though, is more than that. I am a "fixer", so I want to be able to change the situation rather than just control my reaction to it. The quest to find the mechanism for this change is what led to this book.

As I explain in greater detail in chapter 8, my wife and I were working on our relationship, as many couples do. Through that process, I started to learn things that struck me as incredibly powerful for changing relationship dynamics which ultimately became the ideas in this book.

Using these ideas, I was able to start to change my behavior by changing the basis of my reactions. Through shifting *my* behavior, I was giving my wife a different version of me to interact with, which lead to *her* behavior changing, as well. She was also doing her own work, but we started to interact differently, which opened space for us to work *through* things together rather than *against* each other in them.

As I continued on that path with my wife, I started to notice a pattern with people I was coaching where similar stories were emerging about how we react to others based on what we presume their intentions to be given how they are acting. This leads to avoidance, arguments and frustration at best, and divorce, firings and estrangement at worst.

I decided this was important to share, and started to work on an article for *Inc Magazine*, which I was a contributor to at the time. After writing something ten-times longer than what my editors tend to like and still feeling like I hadn't yet scratched the surface, I realized that there was far more to say about all of this than could fit into a single article. I decided to write a multi-article series for my own blog about this approach to making our various relationships work better. As I got deeper into that approach, I found this was far bigger than even *that* medium would do justice to. It was clear to me that a book was needed.

While *Do a Day* addresses our relationship with ourselves, this book is for the next step—our relationship with others. There are so many "others" in our lives, and so many different nuances to these relationships, whether they are positive or have some level of dysfunction in them. *The 50 75 100 Solution* will teach you the tools and ways to use them to change your role in these relationships to change their dynamic for the better.

My response to the other party in these difficult situations has always been one of judgments, such as:

"Why is she doing this to me?"

"Why can't he just appreciate what I did instead of giving me a hard time?"

"Why am I being punished?"

"Why won't she just love me?"

"Why can't dealing with them just be easier?"

Essentially, I became filled with a chorus of "Why?," placing responsibility elsewhere instead of focusing it internally. This would, in turn, create feelings of failure to move these immovable people.

I kept waiting for the "he," "she," or "they," tied to those questions of "Why?" to change.

I would say things like "If I can just do *this*, then they will be better to me," or "If they would just get help for their issues, our problems would go away," or "If this person leaves the company, then everything will be fine."

The thing about that is, waiting for someone to just start being good to you is like waiting to win the lottery when you haven't even bought a ticket. You may save the effort and expense of buying the ticket, but I guarantee that you will never win.

It's important to pause on the word "win" for a moment. To win does not mean that your side prevails, that you are right or that the other person loses or is wrong. It simply means that the battle has ended and you are still standing. It means that harmony is found.

So if we can't simply expect others to just stop being bad to us, there basically is no hope, right? We cannot force people to change, nor can we expect them to change spontaneously and simply wake up to how great we are. We cannot win.

We might as well give up. Right?

Of course not!

There is a path to changing this, and the answer lies fully within *you* rather than *them*. Through this book, you will learn what *The 50 75 100 Solution* is, why it is so powerful and how you can use it to remove dysfunction from your relationships, while finding inspiration through a happier, more peaceful existence overall.

We tend to focus on worrying about who is at fault, and often don't see that person being ourselves. *The 50 75 100 Solution* comes from the idea that, even if you aren't the cause of the issue, you can still be the source of the solution. Said another way, look at yourself as the one at fault in all situations so you can see the value in changing yourself to fix things. Working on your own part of any problem is the path to making that problem better.

It may sound silly to some, or perhaps impossible or overly simple to others.

It *is* simple, but it is neither silly nor impossible. I know in the same way I know that *Do a Day* works.

I have lived *50 75 100* myself as you'll find throughout the examples I share in this book. Through it, I have been able to transform some of the most difficult relationships I could have imagined into positive ones. And where the relationship didn't change, I stopped seeing myself as a victim of the problem so that a universal solution could be found that benefited me instead of punishing me as part of the issue.

For other relationships, it is working, but the work continues and that is okay. The thing about life is that we are never done growing, changing and working on what is possible. Embrace it. Do not be afraid of or discouraged by the idea that something could be a long-term effort.

With this book, like with *Do a Day*, I will show you how you, too, can find this path I discovered to improve your life. While *Do a Day* was about your relationship with yourself, *The 50 75 100 Solution* is about your relationships with others. I share the ideas that you can use to change relationship dynamics, and then share specific relationship types so you can see how to apply these ideas in real life. At the end of each chapter, I invite you to "Do the Math" by summing up the key points for you to be sure you've understood the message so you can move forward.

But first, a bit more background before we jump in.

Do the Math

- Despite success or happiness in certain areas of our lives, we all have relationships that are difficult and can take away from the happiness we build elsewhere.

- One solution to dealing with tough relationships is to not let them affect us, like water rolling off a duck's back. As much as that is true, to make those relationships less difficult, or even good, would be a better solution.

- Through recognizing your role not just in the relationship's problems but in their solution, you unlock a path to removing dysfunction from your toughest relationships and opening them up to being positive, productive, supportive ones. That idea is the purpose of *The 50 75 100 Solution*.

1.

What Am I Doing Here?

Why am I writing this book? What do I know about the subject of relationship dysfunction and how to resolve it?

The answer is simple. Like you (and most people, really), I have lots of experience with difficult relationships. I have encountered them at home, at work, with friends and more; and there has always been one consistent cause in my mind—someone else.

Yes. That's right.

As far as I was concerned, I was never the root cause of the issue, the one at fault. It was always someone else acting irrationally, maliciously, ignorantly, etc. *They* were all doing something *to me*.

In the rare cases where I started it, I was still right, so it didn't mean that I was at fault despite the issue starting with my actions or words. The ends (my correctness) justified the means (my behavior).

While some of you may judge me for the above confession, I bet many more of you are seeing yourselves in these words (whether you want to admit it openly or not).

I didn't actually think this way all the time; but generally, this is how I have historically looked at dysfunction in my relationships.

That is, I saw the problem as *external* to me. That means that it did not matter what I did, since the problem was not emanating from within me. Since the other person was the true source of the problem, my behavior could not make it better or worse. I was absolved of any and all responsibility for my part in the relationship problem.

The relationship that has been the toughest for me, as I am sure it is for many people, is the one I have with my wife.

Marriage is amazing *and* tough. We get married with good intentions and lots of love, and the challenges we face in life can make it hard to always act in accordance with those intentions and that love. Responsibilities increase and add pressure. Parenting can be stressful and add points of disagreement. Work stress comes home frequently. Financial pressures agitate life. And, yes, we do change. We get married at different points in our lives, and we evolve and adapt, which means our beliefs, approaches, resiliency and many other factors can, and do, change. We also do not go into marriage as clean slates. We come with backstories, baggage, trauma, emotional responses as well as many minor things, such as which way the toilet paper roll should hang (luckily, my wife and I were raised the same, correct way, with it coming down the front rather than falling down the back, which is, of course, wrong).

In my marriage, I can guarantee you that my wife was thinking all the same things I thought at the beginning of this chapter. When we would discuss difficulties in our relationship, her position was very one-sided, with the reason for the dysfunction resting solely or at least primarily on my shoulders. And when she would try to talk about having a hand in it, it never rang true, or at least was couched as being in response to how I was acting or due to the emotional state she was in as a result of my behavior. Of course, I was feeling the exact same thing, but with the players reversed.

When both sides are certain that the other person is primarily, if not entirely, at fault, it is unlikely that you will reach resolution.

While the same dynamic can play out in other difficult relationships, our family relationships are always intensified versions of these dysfunctional interactions because of the frequency, closeness, emotions and consequences at play.

There came a point in my marriage, where my wife and I thought there was no fixing things. We would either coexist as best we could for the sake of our family, or we would end up separating. As a child of divorce, I did not want that for my family. And when I *knew* it was *she* who was causing so much of our dysfunction but was refusing to acknowledge or fix her faults, it became even more frustrating and upsetting. And, of course, her mind was filled with the same idea, but with the players flipped.

At my wife's insistence, I sought help. From her perspective, I needed help to stop being such a monster. From my perspective, I needed help coping with her being so unsupportive, unappreciative, judgmental and mean to me.

It turned out, we were both right in why I should get help. Neither of us knew it at the time.

I started to see a therapist, who happened to be a student of Buddhism. While she helped me directly by talking through a lot of what I was feeling, she suggested I read a few books to help me with how I was choosing to respond to my wife.

Ultimately, my therapist explained, no matter what we face, how it impacts us is *our* choice. That can be hard to take or hard to understand, so let me break it down through an example.

As a kid, I was obese. I got made fun of a lot, though mostly by one of my sisters (we were pretty bad to each other a lot of the time, as many kids close in age can be). For some reason, when some other kid called me a fat name, it did not hurt that much. I basically blew it off, but when my sister called me the same name, it would bring me to tears, or bring me to the kitchen cupboards to seek solace in food (the reason I was overweight to begin with, food was my emotional support, starting with my parents' divorce and increasing as I felt anxiety throughout my childhood). Of course, that only led to her having more of a reason to call me those names, so the cycle self-perpetuated.

The question, though, is why the same words from one person hurt so much more than from someone else?

Simple: *I* let them hurt more. I chose to ignore or not let in the hurtful words from one, and brought in, ruminated on and felt attacked by those same hurtful words from another.

I was making them hurt me.

You will notice my word choice here: "making," as opposed to "letting."

Making is active, while *letting* is more passive; this is an appropriate distinction because I really was doing this and not simply allowing it to happen. That doesn't mean my sister was being nice, she was in deed being cruel. What it means is that, regardless of her actions, I was choosing to be hurt when I had proven to others that I did not have to.

The word "choose" here may feel inaccurate, or perhaps even offensive. Let me clarify.

It may not be a conscious choice, you likely do not sit there when you hear something mean and actively say to yourself, "Hmm... I think I will choose to be offended by that. Yes, that sounds good, let me do that. I will be offended now." Yet that is basically what is going on subconsciously.

With every stimulus we receive, our brain processes what it perceives and decides how to respond. It may be unconscious or seem impossible to control, but actually, we can control these decisions. We can learn to make these split-second choices intentionally or, more accurately, we can *rewire* the way we make them subconsciously through reflection and practice.

Fast-forward to my marriage. When I would do something to try to ease the physical burden on my wife, who suffers from a chronic illness, she would sometimes get angry with me. She would either get upset because I have done it wrong somehow or contrary to what she was planning to do, or, more frequently, I was doing it for a manipulative or mean reason (or at least that is how I took her meaning).

She would either say it was because I must be trying to get pity by showing that I have to do everything and thus I have it so hard, or that I am trying to make her feel incapable, lazy or like a child. Regardless of which judgment she chose, she assumed some malintent or incompetence on my part and would snap at me.

I would then get angry and snap back. I would often try to say I was trying to help her, which she would laugh at and insist otherwise. I would then feel invalidated and judged as bad when I was intending to do good from a place of caring. Then I'd judge her response and feel even worse, getting angrier.

And of course, to her, I really *was* bad, *did* do this thing wrong or for negative reasons, and now was also yelling. In front of our son. And because she believed she was right in her assessment of my motives; she was unable to understand her hand in the bad situation. Even if she was aware of her actions, they were justified since hers were "right" and mine were "wrong." And with all of *that* swirling in my head, I got even angrier and behaved even worse. All of this in front of our son.

This pattern repeated itself on a daily basis, sometimes multiple times a day, and this is what I talked to my therapist about.

The therapist's response, and what she thought I would get from the books she recommended, centered on how I was *choosing* to respond. I *chose* to be attacked rather than see how my wife might have felt wronged or hurt and was simply acting from a place of hurt.

I *chose* to engage in the back and forth. I *chose* to raise my voice, look annoyed, argue, defend myself, etc. I felt the emotions kick in, and then I would act in accordance with them.

But did I have to? Did that response ever help?

No. Literally never. The therapist tried to help me see how to feel what I was feeling, acknowledge and allow that without allowing it to come out, saying to myself, "Wow. That is not what I meant by this at all. I am really surprised by this right now, and hurt too," then going on to say to myself, "Lashing out certainly will not make this bad situation better. I need to do differently."

Finally, I would need to validate what my wife was feeling and apologize meaningfully. A useful and validating apology would be something such as, "I understand how it was hurtful that I stepped in without considering what you wanted, and I can see why that would feel disempowered or as if you were being trampled on. I'm sorry I stepped in without considering what you wanted."

This is far better than my typical apology of something like, "I'm sorry you feel that way." That type of apology, if you can call it that, puts it back on her by passive-aggressively implying that, rather than there being any issue with the actions that elicited her feelings, her feelings are simply wrong.

After my apology, I would need to let her go with whatever she is saying the solution is, taking over from me after I messed up, for example. Instead, I would usually stubbornly resist letting her step in to right my wrong, which would only make it worse.

The key is that the process of changing the dynamic takes time. Changing my behavior one time would not suddenly result in never having issues again, especially if the norm for the relationship is a coexistence intermixed with arguing. I would need to work at it consistently to build a new pattern for both of us.

While my therapist's suggestion of apology is right and does work, it was not new advice for me; it was hard for me to sustain in the past, however, because I was still feeling attacked and wronged. This approach felt like always saying I was wrong in every situation and letting the other person "win."

While the giver of the advice's version of winning was really about creating fewer or shorter fights (or both), which is good, it did not *feel* good to me. I do not generally like the idea of stifling or hiding my emotions, and that is exactly how it felt to me. I was essentially invalidating my own emotions.

I decided to pick up the books the therapist had suggested because I felt a strong need for more and better answers. I wanted a way to really change the game that would make me happier, not just make it so I made others less unhappy by eating their unhappiness myself.

The first book I read was *Open Heart, Clear Mind: An Introduction to the Buddha's Teachings* by Thubten Chodron.[1] She is a Buddhist monk who has written many books on Buddhism, including one she co-authored with His Holiness the 14th Dalai Lama. She walks the reader through the basic principles of Buddhism in an easy-to-understand format that I found enlightening and beautiful. More importantly, I found it immediately inspiring in a very clear way. While reading just a few chapters of the book, I found myself overcome by a sense of how to make things better through the teachings of Buddhism.

I had two major relationship challenges after I was just about a quarter of the way into the book, one at home and one at work. My marriage was on the brink of ruin from the constant fighting, and a colleague at work was attacking me in an attempt to get me fired before I exposed a major failure of her own (more on this story in the chapter *Work*).

I decided, despite being so new to the ideas, that I would apply them. In both cases, the impact was dramatic and fairly immediate. With my coworker, it took one meeting

---

[1] Aavailable at http://www.5075100.com/ohcm

(the one she had called where she was going to take me down), and with my wife it took about two weeks of consistent application on my part.

In seeing how these situations played out, it became clear to me that there is a solution to relationship dysfunction that goes far beyond acquiescing, placating, swallowing your pride or avoiding conflict. Those things all create internal conflict and pain despite what they may or may not do for the relationship.

I had found a path to not only ending the conflict but being happy myself, even in the face of attacks, threats or challenges.

What became clear to me are two dichotomies within dysfunctional relationships: one splitting the situation in half, the other splitting each of those halves in half again, creating four quarters.

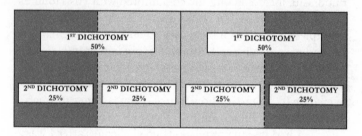

No matter what our role, peer, spouse, customer, subordinate, parent, service provider, etc., and no matter what we are saying or doing in the dysfunction, we own half of the dysfunction. There are two sides to every story, and one of them is ours.

That is the first dichotomy.

The second split comes *within* us. Half of what happens within us is our outward actions; what we say and do to or toward the other person. The other half is our response to them; what we think and feel based on their words and actions. These two halves are connected, as our thoughts and feelings directly lead to our actions and reactions.

Because those halves are within us, that means there is choice involved, choice which *we* control. That does not mean it is easy, nor does it mean it is a conscious choice. Yet these halves of us are the results of our choices in the situation.

As for the "they" in the situation, whoever they may be on the other side of the dysfunctional relationship, this is the other half of the first dichotomy. And that other person exists with the same second dichotomy that we had, but within *them* this time. Half of them is their actions and words directed toward us, and the other half is how they perceive and process what we are doing.

The relationship itself is made up of two halves, us and them, which are themselves made up of two halves, what we do and how we interpret the actions of the other person.

This is the basis of *The 50 75 100 Solution*.

You own 50% of the dysfunction (the "*50*" in the name). Since half of the other person is based on their feelings about your behavior, you *indirectly* have input and influence into another twenty-five percent of the dysfunction (half of their half).

Your 50% plus their 25% gives each of you 75%, of course, which is where the middle number comes from. That means you control or have sway over three-quarters of the dysfunction.

That, to me, is an incredibly empowering realization that can create great hope for solving the issue.

When you can fix 75% of a problem, it is not long until 100% of the dysfunction is better. Hence the final number in the name of the approach.

Do not worry if you just got lost in the math or all the halves you and they are splitting into. There is so much more to share to help you understand this idea and see how to apply it across any dysfunction you face in your life.

One word of caution before we explore deeper. Some relationships may not be able to be fixed with this approach due to very real sources of dysfunction that require proper, professional help.

Four specific issues I would name directly are substance abuse or addiction, physical or mental abuse, criminal behavior, and true mental illness. That does not mean you throw around labels like "crazy" or "alcoholic" nonchalantly to get out of taking responsibility for your hand in a problem; but when the issue is genuine, while it may help you cope better, the approach I share in this book is not appropriate or sufficient.

If someone is genuinely sick or acting dangerously or against the law, please help them seek professional help or consider turning to the authorities. In short, do not compromise your safety or the safety of others in these extreme cases.

Do the Math

- As a "fixer" I was never happy with ignoring the difficult relationships in my life. I wanted to try to change the dynamic into one that was healthy and positive.

- All relationships have two sides to them, each of us sits on one of those sides and needs to take responsibility for our role in the relationship and how it plays out. We can see this responsibility as a form of power to affect change on the other half of the relationship.

- We affect that change through what we put out into the relationship dynamic, through our actions and reactions, giving the other person different inputs to process and respond to. That is, we indirectly influence their behavior through our own. Recognizing this opens us up to seeing how to make the relationship better.

- For situations of true mental illness, violence, addiction or other serious issues that require true professional help, please do seek that help.

II. A FOUNDATION FROM BUDDHISM

To understand *The 50 75 100 Solution*, we first need to explore one of the oldest philosophies in the world, Buddhism.

I say "philosophies" because, while Buddhism is also a religion, you need not follow the religion of Buddhism to understand and follow the philosophies of the *Dharma*, the teachings of the Buddha. You do not need to accept Buddha as your god, believe in Nirvana, reincarnation or anything else you may feel is at odds with your current religious beliefs. Buddhism is extremely accepting of other religions, and many religious leaders from other faiths have studied Buddhism and shared its message on love, the human condition and ending suffering.

It is important to be clear that I am not a Buddhist, a monk nor an expert on Buddhism. I have been studying Buddhism and welcoming the ideas within it into my life, and seek to share what I have come to understand with you. If you wish to learn more about Buddhism, I encourage you to do so, and would recommend starting with Thubten

Chodron's *Open Heart, Clear Mind* or *Buddhism for Beginners*.[2] Both are easy-to-follow introductions to the ideas of Buddhism without any attempt to convert you to a different religion or force feed anything to you.

Chodron uses the analogy of an all-you-can-eat buffet in *Open Heart, Clear Mind* to share how you can choose some ideas while not choosing others that do not appeal to you, just as you would pick some items and avoid others at a buffet. You can always come back for more if you wish, or decide you are full enough with what you have already had.

And while you need not follow the religion of Buddhism to follow the philosophies, you do need to understand and follow three of its core principles to unlock the power of *The 50 75 100 Solution*.

We will take these three key ideas from Buddhism I believe are critical to improving relationship dynamics in turn, to give you the foundation upon which to learn and be able to use *The 50 75 100 Solution*. They are:

1. Happiness Seeking.
2. Interdependence.
3. Impermanence.

In *Open Heart, Clear Mind*, Chodron shares very clearly and beautifully how this all comes together to remove hostility. She says that "a kind heart is the essential cause of happiness... When we respect others and are considerate of their needs, opinions and wishes, hostility evaporates. It takes two people to fight, and if we refuse to be one of them, there is no quarrel."[3]

Let's understand more how we can respect others and their needs, and what we can do with that respect to

---

[2] Available at http://www.5075100.com/buddhismforbeginners

[3] Chodron, Thubten, *Open Heart, Clear Mind*, Snow Lion, Boston, MA, pg. 75–76.

make hostility evaporate, as she puts it, by starting with Happiness Seeking.

Do the Math

- The foundation of *The 50 75 100 Solution* comes from Buddhism, which is ultimately focused on reducing suffering for every living being in the world. Difficult relationships and the fights that typify them are forms of suffering, so of course Buddhism holds keys to solving these tough areas of our lives.

- The three mechanisms to shift tough relationships are:
  1. Happiness Seeking.
  2. Interdependence.
  3. Impermanence.

- Learning how to use these three concepts actively will allow you to bring *The 50 75 100 Solution* into your toughest relationships and shift the dynamics within them.

2.

Happiness Seeking

This is, for me, the most useful of the key aspects when you are in the midst of dealing with a tough relationship. I actively remind myself that this is ultimately what is at play for everyone, the universal desire to be happy.

Human beings, or, actually, any living thing, just want to be happy. We act in a direction we believe will move us toward that. Those actions may have consequences that reduce the Happiness of others, but our general purpose is Happiness for ourselves.

Some people act in ways that reduce their Happiness, but this is really an issue of confusion around what will bring them Happiness or perhaps the outcomes of their behavior being different from what they are expecting.

It is not, however, that they are intentionally acting against their own Happiness. For some, they may act in purposely self-harming ways, which would seem to go against Happiness Seeking, but actually they have some other, greater pain that they believe will be lessened by their self-destructive behavior. For example, someone who is tormented by depression and pain may choose to end their life because the ceasing of their depression is what they believe will make them happy, and they see no other way to do so.

Let me share some other examples that may seem rooted in malicious intent to help show how this Happiness Seeking paradigm is really constantly and universally at play. Once we understand that the pursuit of personal Happiness is what really drives us all, we can start to disarm our emotional reaction when we are in a dysfunctional situation.

The first example is one I think everyone with a driver's license has experienced, getting cut off in traffic.

I was driving home from the airport in pretty heavy traffic one day. I noticed a commercial van behind me that suddenly cut out into the lane next to me, moved forward a bit and cut right back into my lane a little too close to me for comfort (and safety). There were two ways I could have reacted to this. I could get upset, honk, yell (though they obviously wouldn't be able to hear me, despite what most upset drivers think when they start yelling at another driver), and try to cut back in front of *them* to teach them a lesson. Or I could just not care.

Before understanding how people all seek to be happy, I would have chosen the first option. I would have gotten all worked up and been no better off. I would not be closer to home and may have even ended up in a car accident. However, now that I understood what really drives behavior like that of the commercial van driver, I actually smiled. I was not merely indifferent, but was strangely happy. I realized I was happy *for the driver of the van.*

It was so important to them to get in front of me, to be one car closer to their destination, that they felt it was worth driving dangerously and putting me one car's length farther from my destination and they did it, they got a car ahead. They must have felt some level of Happiness, or perhaps less anxiety about how late they were running or how far they still had to go through so much traffic.

I realized that the chances that their only motivation was to delay me reaching my destination by a few seconds were slim to none. They were thinking of what would make *them* happier. What they did not realize was the cost their

Happiness pursuit may have for others. Or perhaps they did realize this cost but valued it less than the benefit they perceived for their own gain. Regardless of whether they did this cost-benefit analysis or were simply ignorant to that cost does not mean they did it to hurt anyone, including me.

Realizing this is why I smiled. Someone became happier, and I was not really any worse off. In fact, I got off the highway at the next exit, while they were most likely still stuck in traffic, so clearly I was doing all right despite what I might have interpreted as being hurt before.

What I didn't mention is what kind of commercial van the driver was in, a plumber's van. Perhaps they weren't just thinking of themselves, but rather their customers. Maybe someone's home was being damaged by a burst pipe that the van driver was headed to fix. Perhaps a customer had a medical condition, had no water and was suffering as a result. Who knows what the driver's reason for cutting me off was, but I do know that it didn't really have anything to do with me personally or specifically. And that helps.

Another spin on the same idea is when we do something at a cost to ourselves for the benefit of someone we love. For example, in 2005's *Cinderella Man*, actor Russell Crowe plays James Braddock, a Depression-era boxer who goes through a great career comeback after becoming a "washed-up" fighter who falls on hard times, like most of the US back then. In one of the early scenes, Braddock's kids are extremely hungry, as food is scarce. Upon seeing that they have no other food for the kids nor any money to buy more, Braddock gives them the ham he was about to eat, leaving nothing for himself. He needs that food desperately, given the manual labor he does to try to support his family and how little he's eaten, but putting his children first fills Braddock in a way that eating the ham could not. He doesn't do it because he's irrational or he wants to torture himself. He does it in his pursuit of Happiness.

We simply need the right perspective to realize that.

If you have ever given someone else your coat when they were cold, you were doing the same thing; putting your own physical comfort second to someone else's not because you are sadistic, but because the Happiness you get from helping that person outweighs the Happiness you would get from being warm while they were cold.

It is easy to see Braddock's actions, or your own when you give up your coat, aligning with the pursuit of Happiness, and see it as good. It can be harder to do so with the plumber who cut me off on the highway.

I share these examples of kindness to help you see that there are multiple dynamics at play, and we may simply only be looking at one of them when we pass judgment on people's intent and then react to our *perception* of their intent.

To clarify this further, let's consider a more black-and-white example where one party is happier and the other is much worse off, predatory animals and their prey.

The wolf kills and eats whatever animal it is hunting, such as a sheep, to survive or perhaps feed a den of cubs. The poor sheep loses its life, and perhaps its own offspring are impacted by losing a parent. The farmer who owns the sheep is financially impacted by the kill as well. But I promise you, the wolf did not kill the sheep to orphan lambs or hurt a farm's profitability. It killed the sheep for its own survival. Just like buying ground beef at the supermarket is not an act rooted in killing cows, but rather feeding your family. And I can realize that even as a Vegan.

We all seek to be happy, though sometimes that process comes at the cost of the Happiness of someone or something else, even an extreme cost such as their death. Despite that cost, it still does not mean our reason for our action was to reduce the Happiness of another.

A personal story of mine that illustrates the point more richly involves a coworker who seemed hell-bent on getting me fired. She attacked my credibility, sent nasty emails to our boss filled with factually inaccurate statements about my actions and performance and demanded a meeting for me to answer for myself.

The thing is, none of what she was claiming actually happened. In fact, the problems that were coming up were a result of her actions rather than mine or those of anyone else. I was simply acting to clean up the messes that were arising that she did not want to acknowledge for fear of being blamed.

As difficult as the situation was, I realized she was not blindly trying to get me fired. Instead, she was reacting to what was happening as a result of her own actions. I imagine she was afraid that she would be taken to task for what was going on, which would either mean huge amounts of work for her or perhaps the loss of her job. The more anyone else worked to clean up the mess, the greater risk the truth about its source would come up, and she would be at risk. Rather than waiting for anyone to come after her, she proactively decided to go on the offensive and try to take out the people who stood the greatest chance of exposing her.

I went into the meeting she insisted upon, armed with the facts, but also with a sense of her real intention (even if she was not fully aware of it). When she lobbed a grenade my way, I responded by asking what she was most concerned about given those facts. I was trying to pull out her definition of Happiness to see if we could all work toward delivering on that without a cost to anyone.

I would like to say it was easy, but that would not be true. She was in full attack mode and fought tirelessly and aggressively. But my approach did defuse her enough to move us all forward. And we did so in a way that no one had to pay a price, as she so feared for herself.

I will come back to this example later in the book when I talk about how to use the approach in work situations to give more detail on what I did as I applied *The 50 75 100 Solution* to solve the problem.

You could challenge this idea, of all people seeking to be happy, with examples such as premeditated murder or revenge. Even in those instances, however, I would say that the perpetrator is still seeking their own Happiness, which in this case may involve getting back at someone or taking the life of another. It is not a form of Happiness I would choose or can even necessarily understand, but it is *their* definition of Happiness in that instance, or at least their *understanding* of it at the time. They may be confused about what they want, thus thinking they will be better off for committing the heinous act against another person. Yet none of that means they are acting for a reason other than seeking what they understand to be Happiness through the means they believe will most likely bring it to them.

One other key idea in Buddhism is that our ultimate goal should be to end suffering, any suffering we encounter. The opposite of suffering is happiness, so when we encounter someone *seeking* happiness, we should ourselves take comfort in the idea that they are suffering less. Better still would be to find a path to ending their suffering without increasing that of another person. For example, if one person is starving, do not feed them with food that someone else is depending on to avoid starving themselves. Seek a solution that allows both people to be fed. This is why it is important to try to find a way to reduce the dysfunction in these difficult relationships as dysfunction creates suffering.

Recognizing that everyone ultimately seeks to be happy—just like you—helps us to feel less personally attacked, wronged or singled-out. We, and our own Happiness, may just be standing in the way of the path that other person has understood to be how they will achieve their Happiness.

When you feel attacked or threatened, it can be hard not to attack back. Seeing how, ultimately, the other person just wants what you want—Happiness—helps us to be more present and able to control how we respond. That means we can employ effective tools to disarm the situation and get a better outcome for everyone.

The tool to do that comes from our understanding of how no one is absolutely good or absolutely bad. Instead, rather, we are good or bad in different situations with different people.

That is, we are Interdependent, as we explore next.

Do the Math

- At our core, we all want the same thing in life, to be happy.

- Sometimes, the Happiness of one comes at the expense of another. Sometimes, we perceive someone's intentions to be purely malicious, but the truth is that we just do not see the Happiness they are trying to achieve. These situations lead us to feel attacked, threatened or invalidated, and this to be intentional on the other person's part, when in fact these are byproducts of their attempts to achieve the Happiness they seek.

- Understanding that everyone else just wants to be happy, just like us, can help us let go of the idea that we are being wronged, which helps us to control our tendency to react in a manner that exacerbates relationship issues rather than seeing how we can reduce them.

- Happiness Seeking is the mechanism for us to not only stand down, but look for paths to resolution by recognizing the real, underlying goal of the other person.

3. Interdependence

One of the most important foundational points in Buddhism is the idea of Interdependence. That is, no one is a certain way in and of themselves. They are that way in relation to other people in a given situation. Or, more accurately, they are that way in relation to their *perceptions* of other people in a given situation. No one is all good or all bad. No one is only nice or only mean. We are nice to some people sometimes, and mean to some people sometimes. And of course, we can be mean *and* nice to the same people in different situations.

This is not just about people, but really everything.

Rainy days are not good or bad in and of themselves. They are good for the farmer whose crops have been suffering from a drought, and bad for the people who live along the banks of a river that is flooding.

It is our actions and the interpretation of these actions by others that result in how we are judged to be in a given moment. I am a cook as I make dinner for friends coming over for a meal, and when I am out for a bike ride, I am a cyclist. My role is dependent on my situation and how those I interact with—my dinner guests or people who see me on my bike—view me in that context. I am neither always a cook nor am I always a cyclist.

The same holds for how we are in our relationships. You may find your boss to be harsh and unfair when he or she comes down on a coworker you like about their poor performance. Later, you may see your boss as being a good manager when they call out the underperformance of someone you don't like. This is the same boss exhibiting the same behavior but with different people, so they are seen in a different light for the same action.

Interdependence in why bullies still have friends. It is why we may get turned down for a date by one person while another person is so enamored with us, they hope we ask them out. It is why some people like the taste of a food while others are repulsed by it. The food is neither tasty nor disgusting in and of itself, but rather it is one of those things to someone as a result of their personal perceptions of the flavor and another to someone else. The same food may even go from being disgusting to being tasty to the *same person* as they age and their tastes changes.

For example, most children do not like asparagus while many adults do. Kids tend to think alcohol is terrible-tasting, yet fast-forward a couple of decades, and that same child now chooses to have a glass of wine, or a beer, with dinner as an adult.

In a previous job I had, we used to issue feedback surveys to our customers. When I would read the open-ended commentary about my staff, I would often find myself laughing at the stark conflicting opinions of the same people, often submitted the same day. I remember one staffer in particular who got a comment that said, "He is the worst person I have ever dealt with. If you don't fire him, I will cancel my policy with you." Two hours later, someone submitted another survey about the same person, saying, "He is the nicest, most professional person. I'm so glad he handled my case. You need to make sure he never leaves your company!"

The same person interacting with different customers can result in night-and-day perceptions of similar behavior. The reason for this is the Interdependence at play in each of these situations, which can yield totally different perceptions despite so many of the variables being held constant.

But why does Interdependence matter? How can it help a troubled relationship? Realistically, you cannot simply be someone else in an argument, or make the other person be someone else, as much as we may wish that to be true. We are who we are in that moment, and the moment has come about already. The situation and players in it exist and cannot magically be swapped out for something less contentious mid-stream, right?

Interdependence helps because you do not actually have to change the people or the subject of the disagreement to get a different outcome. You can change something *else* about the disagreement to change the situation, and thereby yield a different outcome. You are you, they are them, and the reason you are arguing is what it is. But *how* you argue— or, more accurately, how you interact with them—can be used to transform how the whole dynamic unfolds.

Interdependence is bigger than just the people or the subject matter. It is about *everything*. Think of the idea in Chaos Theory of the butterfly effect; a butterfly flapping its wings in one part of the world, making a little bit of wind, sets off a chain reaction that results in a hurricane halfway across the globe. If you alter aspects of the situation, Interdependence means that there can be a chain reaction of change.

Does that sound hard to believe, or perhaps easy to refute from experience?

I am sure you can think of an example where you were arguing with someone who you felt was wrong, and when you tried to tell them how they were wrong—that is, you tried to change the situation from being defined by their incorrect idea to your correct one—things only got worse.

That may be, but you were not actually changing the dynamic; you were merely feeding it with more of the same inflammatory input, a.k.a. disagreement. What I am talking about changing is the dynamic itself, not the other person's perceived wrongness.

Think about a time when you realized you were wrong and apologized in a genuine manner (not just saying "I'm sorry you feel that way," but something more like "I'm sorry my actions hurt you"). That can disarm the other person and take the whole situation down a level in intensity.

Or when two children are fighting over who gets to play with a toy; when they break from the "I want it!" "No, I want it!" dynamic and share or play together, the screaming stops (usually, at least; it depends on how over-tired they are).

When we change the dynamic through how we behave—even when we cannot directly change how the other person behaves—we can make a tough interaction easier.

Happiness Seeking is the *reason* to want to change, and Interdependence is the *mechanism* to affect change.

Interdependence is the tool that allows us to change the dynamic, since our altered actions will lead to a different dynamic with anyone with whom we are interdependent.

But, to be willing to do this, we need to feel that there is a point to the effort. We need hope that realizing people's Happiness Seeking intentions are at play and adjusting our behavior to affect a different outcome is worth it in the first place.

That is where Impermanence comes in, which we'll explore next..

Do the Math

- Interdependence is the idea that nothing exists in and of itself. All things exist in relationship to or through the perception of another. This is why some foods are delicious to one person and disgusting to another, why bullies have friends, and why we may have a terrible fight with someone we love dearly and are compassionate to another time. Changes in either player yield changes in the other.

- The Interdependent nature of all things is the mechanism by which we affect change in the other person's behavior in tough relationship situations. If we are different in our behavior, the other person's perception of us, and ultimately their behavior with us, will change because it has to—it is dependent on what we are doing just as we are with them.

- Through the mechanism of Interdependence, you can be the first domino to fall to cause the chain reaction that leads to a different relationship dynamic.

4. Impermanence

The third core idea from Buddhism that forms the basis of *50 75 100* is the notion of Impermanence. That is, things are not always and forever as they are right now. Just like the age-old adage reminds us, "The only constant is change," everything changes no matter what, including people.

The greatest, strongest mountains change as they erode or they push higher as continental plates underneath them collide. The most healthy, strong individuals age and eventually die. Ideas in millennia-old religious texts are reinterpreted. Scientific facts such as a flat earth with a sun rotating around it are debunked as technology and experience evolves. Nothing is one way always and forever.

Everything in the world changes, and everything ultimately stops existing, if not entirely then at least as it is currently. This does not only apply to people and things, but also to thoughts and behaviors. People and the relationships we have with each other are things as well, so they, too, change and evolve.

We often have the easiest time with the idea of Impermanence when it comes to material things. They break, wear out, etc. Ingredients get combined, cooked and transformed into a dish that is not the same as its component ingredients. The final dish itself then changes as we eat and digest it or, actually, it stops existing as that dish and becomes chemicals fueling our body.

Buddhism likely would not argue point quite that way. Instead, it would say that our *perception* of the thing as it was ends, as we can no longer perceive it as we once experienced it. The food is gone, the movie is over, the discussion has ended.

People, however, have a harder time with this notion. In some areas, it's easy. For example, we know people age, change their hairstyle, grow, gain or lose weight, get injured, etc. Or their situation changes: they move, change jobs, get married or divorced, become parents and so on.

In regard of their personalities, though, we tend to think of people in more constant terms. They are good or bad; loving or cold; understanding, compassionate and kind or indignant, stubborn and harsh. But the truth is, no one exists always in the same way, whether physically or emotionally, inwardly or outwardly.

If you are having trouble understanding this, ask yourself: Are you always one way or the other? Do you have your moments? Are you kind to some people and mean to others? Or are you kind and mean to the same person at different times?

Surely you answered yes to each of these questions. So of course you change. And so do others. So do we all.

If you still do not see it, think about a loved one, such as a parent or significant other. Have you only had kind, loving, supportive interactions with that person, always and forever? Have you never fought with them, offended them or been offended by them?

To these questions, I am sure you answered no. Yet despite that, you still love them, right? You feel close to them. You feel loved by them. Without Impermanence, you would not have these two sides (or perhaps more) to the relationship.

And you are not unique, nor is your relationship with that loved one. This is the case for all things throughout the world. Impermanence as applied to personality does not only exist in certain cultures, settings, genders, age groups or any other sub-group. We all change our behaviors in complex ways and for a variety of reasons, both consciously and unconsciously.

This is an incredibly important, foundational notion. On its own, you may accept it on a surface level, yes; but you need to really believe that all things change to be able to employ *The 50 75 100 Solution*. It is a core input into your ability to let go of your role in dysfunction, because Impermanence is the source of hope that you can fix things. Without that hope, you may not be willing to try.

In *Open Heart, Clear Mind*, Chodron uses the ideas of a cracker[4] and a table to really illustrate the dilemma that arises if you insist everything is exactly as it is always.

Starting with the question, "What is a cracker?"

We see that it is a mixture of ingredients, like flour and water, that gets baked and turned into this thing we call a cracker. At what point does it become a cracker and what happens when you eat it? If you bite part of it, is that the cracker, or is the part left behind the cracker? If it is what you left behind, then what are you eating? If it is the portion you ate first, then what is the remaining portion now? Are they both a cracker despite being different now? And what was the thing you *had* called a cracker before taking that bite that you *now* consider to be the cracker (unless you are considering the piece left behind to be the cracker)? And if the original whole is no longer the cracker because it has been replaced in that role by one or both of these parts, what is the past whole cracker now, and where did it go? And once we have eaten the whole thing, we stop thinking about its present state as "cracker", which we reserve for the past tense of what it was before being eaten; but what is inside of us now?

This is not meant to hurt your brain to think about or to be a silly exercise. It is intended to show

---

[4] Chodron, Thubten, *Open Heart, Clear Mind*, pg. 160–163.

Impermanence and how tricky it can be to track our original, stagnant conception of something.

The idea of "cracker" is fluid and changing, rather than discrete, explicit and unchanging. The same idea can be discrete and specific (the thing that comes out of the oven and is still whole) or broad and fluid (the various pieces of the original whole as we eat it and simultaneously still representing the original thing that stopped existing as it once was). This obviously brings Interdependence into play, too, as your judgment or interaction with the cracker is a key to how it changes.

Chodron does the same exercise with the idea of a table. It is made up of legs and a top, and perhaps some other things, like a drawer and a removable leaf to change its size. If the legs break off, what is left? Would you look at the broken table before you and use a new word, or call it a "broken table"? That is, would you still call it a table, even though it's different now and cannot serve the purpose of a table as it is currently? The definition you used to form the idea of "table" no longer applies, yet you still call it a table. And what if the leaf is in place or not? Is it the same table even if it is markedly different in appearance and function since it can seat, say, half as many without the leaf as with it?

These may seem like pointless or even annoying discussions (did you really expect to contemplate the "crackerness" of a cracker?), but the point of this exercise is to show you that everything is complex and changing, and it's really our perceptions of things and how we apply them that change most.

With the cracker, we stopped seeing it as a cracker at some point. With the table, even though it stopped matching the definition we had for it, we may still call it a table (just a broken or unusable one).

But are these situations really any different from each other?

The only difference is the choices we make in how we think about the eaten cracker or broken table. They both change, though our framing of them may be static. Or static in one case and fluid in another.

Recognizing how everything is Impermanent helps tremendously with tough relationships. Someone who is mean to us has the possibility to not be mean. Someone hurting us can stop doing so (please keep in mind my earlier warning about situations where you are in real physical danger and how it is important to seek help). Someone who misunderstands us or our intentions can see the good in us. Just because they do not do any of the things we want them to right now does not mean they never can or never will. All things, including people and their behaviors, change. Or, more accurately, all things have the *capacity* to change.

Remembering Interdependence, we see a path to sparking that change. All people and all of our behaviors are Interdependent on the situation and the players in those situations. Since no behavior is inherently permanent, a change to the situation can yield a change in the unwanted behavior through the chain of Interdependence.

We have hope from Impermanence that a change in our relationship can and will happen, and the mechanism to make that change comes through the Interdependence of all the pieces of the puzzle in a situation.

Going back to Happiness Seeking; we enter a situation, or at least shift our mindset in a tense situation, by reducing our own sense of being attacked and recognizing that the other person is simply trying to be happy. It is just coming at our expense. They are not trying to hurt us merely to hurt us in some sick or cruel way. They want to be happy, just like we do, and for some reason that involves us giving up some or all of our own Happiness.

Thubten Chodron brilliantly sums up the benefit of Impermanence in *Buddhism for Beginners* when she writes, "By eliminating the wrong concept of permanence and the disturbing attitudes that stem from it, our minds will become

clearer and we'll be able to enjoy things for what they are…
We will not be so touchy about how others treat us."[5]

[5] Chodron, Thubten, *Buddhism for Beginners*, Snow Lion, Boston, MA, pg. 40.

Do the Math

- Impermanence is the idea that all things change in this world. Nothing is the same way forever, including people and how we behave and interact. While we know this to be true objectively, in heated moments we can lose sight of this idea.

- Impermanence also allows us to see the other person in a more positive way because we recognize that our fixed, negative view of them or their behavior is not necessarily accurate. They may be "bad" at the moment, but that does not mean they must always be "bad". In this way, we are sort of adding to Happiness Seeking by recognizing another good thing in them; not only do they wish to be happy like we do, but they also have the capacity to grow, change and improve, just as we can.

- Impermanence gives us hope in tough relationships that the efforts we make from recognizing that the other person is seeking to be happy, just like us, and a shift in our behavior can cause a shift in theirs because nothing is permanent. They can change, just as we are seeking to change ourselves. If not, our efforts would not be worth it. Impermanence reassures us of the value of the whole endeavor, and helps us to hold on through the tough moments while we do the work because we know a change is coming.

III. THE 50 75 100 SOLUTION

With all this background, it's now time to understand what these numbers "50, 75 and 100" mean, and how they can be the solution for any relationship difficulties you face. It is as powerful as it is simple, but that simplicity and power rests in your ability to accept and practice it fully and unwaveringly. Therein lies your ability to remove dysfunction and strife to make any relationship healthier and more successful.

What is *The 50 75 100 Solution*?

Quite simply, it is a way to recognize how much power you have in any difficult interaction or relationship (the "*50 75 100*" part of the name). Once you understand your power, you can use it to affect a more positive dynamic in the relationship or interaction (the "Solution" part of the name).

The power the solution speaks to is the ability to redefine the dynamic by shifting your attitude and taking responsibility for your ability to affect change. You may not be the source of the problem (or may not see yourself to be), yet you can still be the source of the solution. While we often care greatly about who is to blame and get stuck in trying to prove where the true fault lies, it is far better to focus on who to *thank* for solving a problem as that is what moves us forward.

The numbers refer to percentages of the whole relationship; namely, half, three quarters and the entire relationship dynamic. In reality, while we start with fifty-percent, the underlying unit we will work with is quarters of the whole, as you will soon see. There is an interesting and powerful mirror image at play across the two actors in any relationship that creates the mechanism for *The 50 75 100 Solution* to work.

While the discussion of the solution is written from the perspective of two individual actors, it applies more broadly to any relationships, regardless of how many people are involved, such as a multi-person family or interactions between two opposing groups, such as a labor negotiation between management and a union. It also applies when one side is singular and the other is plural, such as when you might try to resolve an issue you have with a group of people.

The reason is simple, when you realize your contribution to the dynamic and the way that can influence the contribution of the other side, you can make change. That is true when the "you" in that phrase is literally just you, or when that "you" is a word representing a group you are part of. And it is true whether the other actor in the relationship is one or many.

Before we jump into the solution directly, I want to reiterate the word of caution I raised earlier. It is important to note that there are situations where *50 75 100* may not work, or more accurately, it would not be appropriate or recommended.

Specific situations would be where either individual suffers from mental illness or is in the throes of addiction, or where real physical harm or the credible threat of harm is present. While the solution may still work and can certainly be a source of compassion and support from you to help the other person through their struggles, it may not resolve this conflict and may put someone at material risk.

In these situations, it is important to seek professional help. That said, it is equally important not to give up on the approach or write a relationship off as being broken because the other person is "crazy" or "sick". It is important to differentiate between dismissive or spiteful labeling in the heat of an argument and true illness or danger. Apply the right understanding of the situation rather than rushing to use labels that seemingly let you or the other person off the hook to do the self-work you know is right.

Do the Math

- All relationships are made up of the pieces of the whole that each of the players contributes to the situation. This is the basis for our responsibilities in the relationship and our ability to guide the relationship.

- When you reflect on how these pieces come together, you find the path to take the three core ideas from Buddhism and use them to shift tough relationships.

- It is important to realize this is not just about two-person disputes, but any relationship between two sides, whether that involves only individuals or groups of individuals. It is also important to remember that professional help may be needed in extreme situations such as those where physical harm is a possibility.

5.

50: Your Half of the Equation

Let's begin by understanding the first number, "*50.*" This is the percent of any relationship or interaction that you directly own. No matter who is in charge or subordinate, speaks or is silent, raises their voice or speaks calmly, is older or younger, is the parent or the child, has transgressed or is innocent, we all are half of any two-sided relationship. You own 50%, as does the other person.

However, within your 50%, you are divided again in half. Half of you is your actions; what you actively and independently choose to put out into the world.

That is, these are the things you say and do, think and feel independent of what the other person is doing. The other half of your side of the equation is your reactions; what you say, do, think and feel in response to the actions and words of the other person. These can manifest as verbal comebacks, hitting them, throwing something at them, dropping your jaw in shock, crying, being offended or angry, storming off or some other reactionary behavior.

To put it simply, you are split between how you act and react in relation to internal and external forces at play on your thoughts and behaviors.

We generally view our actions as a choice under our control. We decide what we are going to say to open a discussion: how we are going to walk into a room, whether we will use a loud or soft voice, whether we are going to drive aggressively and never let people in front of us, or whether we will be gracious and accommodating to other drivers, etc. Our actions may be tied to other things in our lives, such as whether we are in a good or bad mood, whether we are running late to get somewhere, whether we are sick or tired, etc. But, ultimately, we generally feel more control of what we put out into the world than what we receive from the world.

Because we cannot choose what the world throws at us, by extension, we often view our reactions as not being a choice.

People tend to describe their reactions with phrases such as, "I had no choice but to react as I did because they did X to me." If the other person hits you (literally or figuratively), you have to hit back, right? You did not choose for them to hit you, so you clearly did not choose to hit them back. It just happened as it was supposed to. They chose, and you responded accordingly. And that hit hurt you, didn't it? Of course, you did not choose for it to hurt or bother you, that is just what being hit – which was out of your control – did to you personally – which was also out of your control.

The flaw in that thinking is in missing that you still have a choice. You may not choose what is sent your way by other people, but you can still choose whether you respond in kind or turn the other cheek. You can choose whether you allow it to affect or hurt you. If I call you a name, it is up to you how you process that name, whether you let it offend you, and whether you engage with me or walk away.

The word "choice" here often offends people when I say it. They feel I'm both blaming them for something they did not choose *and* am failing to recognize how hard it is for them to choose not to respond given how seriously they were wronged.

Having a choice does not mean it is easy to exercise that choice. What we take from others can be incredibly difficult, hurtful and painful. No one is saying it is always easy to choose a better response but being difficult does not mean you do not have the freedom to choose anyway. It just means you have to work that much harder to exercise it.

To be willing to do that, you have to value the potential better outcome and see there being a chance at arriving at that better outcome if you do exercise your choice in the situation.

Sometimes, the path to exercising that choice may require you to step back or step away, giving yourself a time out. At times, and especially in heated interactions, we can become flooded emotionally, causing us to react rather than respond helpfully because we are in a state of fight, flight or freeze. That can render us unable to think through how to respond appropriately. Giving ourselves this momentary break can make the space for a more productive thought process and interactive approach.

Giving yourself the space to think is where the Buddhist ideas can start to help.

Remembering that the other person is seeking their definition of Happiness rather than only seeking to do us harm helps disarm us in a heated situation and gives us the room to try to exercise our choice of a healthier reaction.

Interdependence reminds us that changing something about the dynamic on our side of the equation can yield a different behavior on the other person's part.

Impermanence gives us hope that, just like everything else in life, their behavior can change or at least the way their behavior *impacts* us can change. Even if they are doing the same thing again, that does not mean it hurts or influences us in the same way.

So, we own half of the equation, and within us, we are a mix of our freely-chosen, independently-decided actions and our dependently-chosen reactions to what the other person is saying and doing. We have complete control over what we put out into the world via these actions and reaction, even if exercising that control may be hard at times.

And in the other person, this same dichotomy exists. They are responsible for half of the relationship. And within that, half of their contribution is actively in them, and the other half exists in response to you. They are a mirror image of you.

If we are having a difficult interaction with someone, we can get stuck at a fifty-fifty stalemate position, and reach an impasse. This can be in arguments, negotiations or any situation where we are not getting along well. Once we recognize that they have the same split within them that we have within us, we see a path to *75*.

Do the Math

- In any relationship, we are responsible for our half of the situation. This is the 50, and it refers to the 50% we are responsible for. The same is true for the other person in that they also have 50% of the equation.

- Within our half, we are split again between what we freely choose to put out into the world through our actions, and how we react to what we take in from the world, including the other person in the relationship.

- Our half is not unique, with the other person having the exact same dynamic within them. Half of their 50% is based on their actions, and half is in response to what they are taking in from us.

- In this way, the whole relationship can be thought of as the sum of four quarters; two from our 50%, and two from the other person's.

6.

75: Your Control & Influence

The next number, *75*, comes from our recognition that the other person has the same split within them that we have within our half of the equation. Understanding this unlocks something you may not realize you have in these difficult relationships – influence. More specifically, you have influence over how the other person is acting and reaction.

We have control over our half of the argument. And we feel that we have no control over the other person. This is why it is hard to exercise our choice in how we react. However, while we may lack actual control of their behavior, we have a strong influence over them through the mechanism of their reactions.

Remember, their reactions are how they respond to what we are putting out to them through our own actions and reactions. That means if we give them something different to process, they may respond in a different, less hurtful or heated manner. It also means that they can exercise their choice in how they respond, and by giving them something less inflammatory that aligns better to the Happiness they are seeking, we can trigger a less inflammatory reaction from them.

As we have already discussed, the choice of having a less difficult reaction can be a hard one to make, so if we give them something less aggressive, attacking, threatening or blocking to their pursuit of the Happiness they are seeking, we make the choice easier for them to make. We start to influence their behavior.

If someone is arguing with you because they see you as a threat, and you respond to their harshness in kind, you are validating their concern and giving them reason to keep attacking or perhaps even increase the severity of their attacks. If, however, you realize what is going on and react in a non-threatening way, that lets them see a clearer path to the Happiness they are seeking, you may start to see a different set of behaviors from them.

A great example is when you get reprimanded by an authority figure, such as a police officer or a teacher in school. They feel you have done something wrong, and expect you to behave insubordinately since you are, in their eyes, a wrong-doer. The easiest way to get them to stop coming at you hard is to comply. They are not expecting this since they have defined you as "bad", so exhibiting good behavior will often make them stop, perhaps confuse them a bit, and change tact.

Growing up, one of my sisters used to pick on me incessantly about my weight. She knew where my buttons were and exactly how to push them. It always hurt so much, and I would react just as she wanted me to – by being upset, crying, trying to defend myself, etc. Everyone told me to just ignore her. That never made sense to me since she was saying hurtful things, and I could hear them. If I could hear them, they hurt. How could I ignore that?

But they were right.

Yes, it hurt, but whether I allowed that hurt to define my reaction was up to me, hard as that may have seemed at the time. And if I could control it, I would not react as she expected (and hoped), and I would not egg her on to keep doing it. She would not get what she wanted, and would eventually give up that approach.

I won't say I succeeded as a child in doing that, but I have kept that advice in mind as I have grown up and have used it to shockingly good effect.

Ignoring the person antagonizing me (or, more accurately, not letting myself respond in a way that shows that I am bothered) almost always gets the person to back off and find another target, or stop completely.

I choose to control my reaction, which changes what they are taking in from me, changing what they then decided to put out into the world for me to process and respond to. By seeing my influence over their reactions and choosing to do something different to influence a change in their behavior, I have been able to change the unhealthy dynamic we would otherwise stay caught in.

Do the Math

- Within our 50% of the relationship, we can choose to act and react differently. By trying to understand the Happiness the other person is seeking, we feel less attacked, and respond in less attacking or defensive ways.

- Through Interdependence, when we reduce or eliminate the destructive patterns within our actions and reactions, we are feeding the reactive part of the other person with new stimuli that is less likely to spark a defensive or attacking response from them. This creates a virtuous cycle that will almost automatically turn down the heat, which will let the boiling water between us start to cool.

- As we do better with our half, and influence a less unhealthy response from the other person's reactive part of their half, three quarters of the relationship move to a healthier place. This sets us up to complete the picture of changing the relationship.

7.

100: Round Up to Better

One Hundred follows directly from *75*. When you control or influence three quarters of a difficult relationship, you can lead it to being 100% better. This may not happen all at once, so it might require you to keep at it and repeatedly respond differently when you are being attacked, mistreated, wronged, etc. Over time, you can start to turn the dynamic around.

With some people, the path to *100* may come in the form of not engaging with them anymore. The "just ignore her" advice I had been given can mean not responding at all, or simply engaging with other people instead. Sometimes, that is the best path, but it obviously does not apply or may not be an option in many situations. I could not choose "not to work with" my sister anymore, so to speak. But I did choose not to play with a neighborhood bully, and if he was around, I just went and did something else.

In relationships where avoiding or ignoring the person is not an option, I have found that repeatedly engaging differently can start to yield results much faster than I expected they would as I started to try. In one very difficult case, I would say that the extremely unhealthy behavior was all but gone after two weeks of nearly daily positive interactions. In another, the other party saw within days that I was not who they thought I was, and started to shift how they were treating me.

What *100* does not mean is that every tough relationship ends up perfect. Just because you no longer attack each other does not mean you are best friends who go around holding hands and smiling at each other. It does not mean that romantic relationships that are falling apart do not end. It does mean, however, that things move forward in a civil manner that is less destructive and hurtful.

If you and a coworker are always attacking each other, the attacks can stop, but that does not mean you will work together on everything by choice and like each other. If your marriage is failing, you may still find yourself divorced, but with a partner you can get along with to co-parent and not bad-mouth each other publicly.

The *100* here may not mean a utopian version of your difficult relationship, and that may suggest it is not all that valuable. Perhaps it is not, but maybe that is asking too much. At least at first.

Think for a moment about your toughest relationship with someone close to you. Maybe it is someone in your family, a coworker, classmate or your significant other. You fight every time you see each other (or it just feels like you do), you have anxiety about seeing them, and you walk away from each interaction upset, drained, hurt and worse off.

What if that stopped? What if you could be on a project together without undermining each other? What if you could live together without feeling constantly cut-down and mistrusted? What if you could go into meetings without feeling humiliated or like someone is trying to get you fired? It may not be utopia, but it is clearly much better than the alternative.

And it is within your reach.

Starting with your half of the equation, you can own what you put out there actively and independently, and how you choose to react to what is being thrown at you.

You start by recognizing the other person is just trying to be happy, just like you are. And, for whatever reason, your Happiness and their Happiness do not seem to be compatible in their eyes right now, and they are acting accordingly. And they may not even be aware of it. And for a little self-awareness, the "they" in this line of thinking could be you, even if you do not see how that is possible. That is at least how the other person feels about it.

When you change what you are putting out into the world for the other person to take in and respond to, you start to influence their behavior because you are both interdependently-connected in this relationship.

If they stop seeing you as standing in the way of, trying to take away or diminish their Happiness, they will start to change the negative way in which they are interacting with you. It may even happen automatically or subconsciously for them as their natural desire to be happy will not be as constrained, so their brain will stop reacting to what it thought was a threat.

By putting out a different set of actions and reactions for them to process, you might be causing them to lower the level of their attack without even knowing they are doing it.

Whether all at once in a single moment, or over time through repeatedly giving them something different to process, you bring about the change in them that everything is susceptible to as everything, even relationships, is impermanent.

Do the Math

- With our half in a better place with less attacking, defending and a general recognition of and support for the Happiness of the other person, we have influenced half of them to move to a better place, too.

- The only piece of the whole to improve then, is the quarter that comes from the actions of the other person. With a healthier dynamic and environment around it, the other person will naturally move to acting in healthier, more supportive or at least less attacking ways.

- This shift in their approach may take time to develop and may require consistent proof from you acting and reacting better than they expect to show them that they are safe to change their actions. Once this happens, all four quarters of the relationship will be operating in a better way, and 100% of the dynamic will be improved.

IV. HOW & WHERE TO USE 50 75 100

With all this background and an understanding of what *The 50 75 100 Solution* is, it is now time to look at some specific situations and contexts in our lives where it can help.

Beyond seeing the situations, we will look at how to use *50 75 100* in these areas through some direct examples and case studies. You may face different situations in your life, but through this study, you will have a better understanding of the solution and how to apply it across your relationships to make them healthier, happier and more positive components of your path forward.

8.

Others of Significance

As you can imagine, this is the hardest part of the book to write for many reasons. First of all, this touches on the relationships closest to us that we spend the most time with throughout our lives. Second, it involves me discussing the other side of the relationship equation without the same sort of protective anonymity that I can when I talk about coworkers or others in my life.

For the same reasons this is a hard section to write, it is also perhaps the most important. Our relationships with our significant others, however that terms plays out in our lives, can be the central problem relationship we face or the center of support for dealing with problems in our other relationships. This is the most core relationship that matters above all others we have beyond our relationship with ourselves.

For me to talk about my relationship with my wife, I should share that it is not perfect. We have ups and downs, as do pretty much all relationships. Sometimes, we have them in the same day, and sometimes we are up for a stretch and down for another stretch.

I am not writing this from a place of everything being perfect always. In fact, I do not think such a place exists for anyone. We are complex, changing beings who are influenced to varying degrees by what we face in life, which means we will have moments that are better and moments that are worse in our relationship with our significant other no matter how much work we do, how good it gets, or how close we are.

And that is ok. You need to be comfortable with the idea that there is no perfect situation and the work never really stops. We learn, evolve and grow together on this journey, and must keep putting in the effort to do so. Embrace that notion, and you can move forward.

With that in mind, I will call back to the earlier discussion where my wife and I were embroiled in a pretty tough, repetitive situation, where we both seemed unable to do anything other than make the other one madder at us. It was in the midst of this that the idea of *The 50 75 100 Solution* was born.

In our dynamic, there are a few negative things that I consistently feel from my wife, and several she consistently feels from me. These feelings are not necessarily tied to either of our intentions, or at least they are not tied to them as consistently as we think they are. That is, we are assuming an ongoing malicious intent. She sees my words and actions as statements about her that I am trying to make, and I do the same with how she treats me.

Specifically, some of the things she has felt from me include that I am not truly supportive of her, think she is making her health issues up, that she is a burden to me and that I resent all of it. There is a lot behind these feelings, and I will say in her defense that I gave her reasons to feel all of it, intentionally and unintentionally.

As I've mentioned here, and in *Do a Day*, I was not the caring, supportive, compassionate husband she needed when her life was in jeopardy in 2011. I was too caught up in my anxiety spiral to be that for her. The way I was behaving gave her the perception that I found her to be a burden and that she was crazy or making things up. I did not seem to have time for her or what she was going through. While I was not thinking or feeling that, I was certainly behaving in a way that was consistent with that read, and it built a perception of me in her that grew and grew.

When we would get into arguments where these feelings would come out, my defense of my intentions and attempts to point out her hand in the situation only reinforced her perception that I was not taking her seriously, seeing my faults and thought she was "crazy" for what she was saying.

I insisted none of that was true, and just went even harder on my defense, which only engrained her feelings further. It was the definition of a vicious cycle.

So what changed in this one big fight where *The Solution* hit me?

As I had been reading *Open Heart, Clear Mind*, I thought about Happiness, and what Happiness my wife was actually seeking. I realized I was focused on the opposite of that, what pain she was seeking to inflict on me through her judgment, behavior and treatment of me. Of course, I only felt more attacked because I was looking at the attack as the intention rather than a perhaps-misguided tool of the pursuit of the Happiness she was trying to get to.

The thing is, I had no idea at the time what she wanted. However, framing my focus on Happiness rather than pain separated out the malicious intent I had been assuming, which made me hurt so much more. And, of course, that hurt lead me to double down on the fight.

If she did not have a malicious intent – to be cruel to me, make me feel unappreciated and incompetent – then she must have an opposite intention. The opposite of a malicious intention is a benevolent one. Obviously, the benevolence was not toward me, so I needed to reflect on who it was for the benefit of, and again Chodron's book helped me to see this as we all seek our definition of Happiness. She was trying to achieve some Happiness for herself.

I could look at this as a selfish thing, and rail against it more, or recognize that we all ultimately just want that, including me. I cannot fairly judge her for wanting to be happy herself when I wanted to be, too. That is hypocritical.

So I knew what her intention was, and who it was for, but I did not know the specific Happiness she was seeking. I needed to understand that to be able to align to it or at least stop standing in the way so she might see me differently.

I realized that the wrong perceptions of me (as I believed them to be) that she held were the clues.

It all harkened back to 2011 when they were established. Everything before and after that was then brought in as evidence to bolster the perception that I was not supportive. And when I looked at how she made me feel, the one thing it all boiled down to is that I felt unsupported. Of course! How could she support me if I do not support her?

It may sound too simple, but the gravity of what support means here is significant since the support she needed from me in 2011 was support to just stay alive, and she felt the opposite from me, so the consequences of my behavior were extremely serious.

This was not just about not being nice or compassionate. My wife has a chronic illness which presented itself in the summer of 2011 and nearly took her life. Our son was just two years old, and had a front-row seat to his mother's decline. While I was doing a lot to support her logistically, I was overcome by my own anxiety, and was working against her emotionally. It was a time I am not proud of, and also a catalyst of a change in me I am very proud of that I talk about extensively in *Do a Day*. While I changed, I hadn't yet in 2011, and given the gravity of the situation, that was incredibly hurtful and dangerous to her.

Quite literally, this was life or death. So me not being supportive also meant she was not safe, which has been a consistent theme for her, and actually for me too as I go back to how I felt when my parents got divorced when I was very young. I understood her differently all of the sudden.

With this realization, I felt that I started to grasp what she was really fighting about, and what I needed to focus on doing to start to let her see that Happiness she sought as possible.

The problem is, I could not do all of this thinking, behavior change and letting her observe and appreciate the change in the middle of this very bad fight. It was late on a Sunday night, I had a 5 a.m. flight the next morning, since I worked out of town all week, and we were at a serious impasse.

What did happen in the middle of all of this is my initial realization that her intention was not simply to be mean to me, and that she did in fact have some Happiness she felt was threatened by me that she desperately wanted to get to.

That was enough for me to know I needed to break the cycle, even if that meant I was "wrong" in the fight or would have to walk away while she shouted more insults or accusations I would normally, desperately want to respond to. Very much against my character and style, I needed to walk away calmly, peacefully, from a place of love.

I let her finish the thought she was on. I nodded. I thanked her for telling me all of that, and said that I think it would be best if we stop here. I told her I loved her, and I was very sorry that I was making her feel any of this, I was going to work on it. I told her I loved her again, said goodnight, and walked away. She said something or other with a mean tone, but I do not know what it was because I basically switched off my brain from listening so that I would not engage because I knew it was pointless at best, and damaging at worst. I walked away, got into bed, meditated on the idea of Happiness Seeking and what Happiness she might be trying to find, and, shockingly to me, I fell asleep.

We spoke very little the next week, as I was on the road, but I made a point of just listening and trying to acknowledge and validate anything she told me. I did not share any of what I was going through, and tried to make our interactions about her situation as much as possible.

When I came home at the end of the week, I kept to the same approach and also stayed acutely aware of my responses and reactions. She was still not happy with me and was still reacting to years of what I had been putting out there for her to process. I made a choice to stop putting out more of it as much as possible.

When I felt myself slipping or getting very triggered by something she would say or do, I reminded myself where her words or actions were really coming from – a benevolent intention for her rather than a malicious intention for me – that helped bring my anger level down enough to react differently. And if I was not able to bring myself back down, I took myself out of the situation, even briefly, to stop from reacting before I could think through it all. She must have thought there was something wrong with me with how many times I said I had to go to the bathroom!

The more consistent I was, the less I received what I would have found to be triggering treatment from her. As a second week of this shifting dynamic ended, I noticed that I had not really been attacked.

This definitely helped to bring us back from the brink. I would love to say there was never another escalation again, but that would not be true, nor would it be helpful to any of you. What I will say is that the more aware I am of her intentions and desires, the less we go toe-to-toe, and when we do, I am able to help steer it back to peace by controlling my behavior. Ultimately, that is all we can be responsible for, so it is about taking your responsibility seriously.

I had a nice reminder of this while writing this book. My wife and I had both been exhausted and worried as our son had been extremely sick for a number of days. We were not sleeping much at all, our hearts were absolutely broken for him, and we both felt helpless in many respects for the seeming inability to break the cycle and get him well.

In TV shows and the movies, you see couples wrapping their arms around each other lovingly as they deal with such situations. In reality, you see two exhausted parents, mountains of used tissues and a general sense that some sort of tropical storm had just been through the house moments ago. In that context, we were both on edge and our short-term memories were essentially non-existent from the sleep deprivation.

I had a meeting to go to on day eight of this ordeal and told my wife I was going to leave early so I could stop at the grocery store to get a few things we needed first. I had to get right home after the meeting as she had somewhere to be, so I could not go afterward. I asked her if she needed anything from the store other than what we went over, and she said she did not.

Fast forward thirty minutes as I went to leave, and in response to me saying, "See you guys at 10:15. Love you!" My wife called out, "Wait, where are you going?"

It was not actually said with a harsh or questioning tone, or at least I know it was not meant that way and likely was not said that way. However, my ears heard differently. I heard, "Wait! *Where* are *you* going?!"

I read malicious intention in these words. I felt questioned and mistrusted. I felt exhausted to have to re-explain something we had already been over. I felt defensive, like I was presumed to be up to something. I felt attacked.

I attacked back. I said, in a stern and angry tone, "I'm going where I already told you I'm going. We went over this. Why are you questioning me?" And my wife, understandably snapped back. We had a bit of a back and forth on it that fit our old pattern, and then we both went silent. I got my coat and keys, and put on my shoes, and realized what I had just done. I had taken in her actions but processed them with feelings from years ago. I had assumed a malicious, untrusting intent, which was not alive or present in that moment, and I reacted from that place.

I lifted my head, turned to her, and said, "I'm sorry. I'm really sorry. I just reacted to past patterns, which is totally unfair to you. You did not do anything wrong. That was wrong of me, and I'm sorry."

She felt validated and supported and thanked me. This is part of not being perfect. It is not that we never fight or argue (and some are much worse than this brief transgression, of course), but the tools are there to repair when we do.

Interestingly, as you practice more, you realize it takes less energy to be this way than to let your anger take over and guide your reactions. It may feel like more work at first as you hold back, think, and act in a way that supports everyone's definition of Happiness, but you soon find that the conscious effort is much less than the mindless, runaway anger approach that expends huge amounts of energy over longer periods of time.

In fact, just the next day after that minor head-butting, my wife became sick, and needed more of me at night, bringing her food in bed. She might have seen me as taking this as a burden before, and I might have felt that she was being insensitive to my needs since I was not in a good place either. But despite being tired and having my own things to do, I realized she just wants to feel better so she can take care of our son and help me, just like me. And she was scared that she was going to be too sick to be there for him, just like me.

I brought her food to her, and laid in bed with her while she ate to keep her company and talk about all the various thoughts we both had on our mind. I would not say it was one of the nicest evenings we have had in a while since she was sick and I was burnt out (though our son was finally on the mend), but it was actually calm, enjoyable and easy. Most importantly, it was a little moment of reinforcement of the good intentions we both have.

I point this out not so much about the specific moment, but that it came on the back of a "bad" one the day before. That rough exchange may not have been ideal, but because we had the tools to do something about it, it allowed for a really nice one shortly after. As I remembered back to that big fight that sparked this whole journey, I know that speed of turnaround from a well-handled bad moment to a good one would not have been possible without this shift. And that is an extremely valuable piece of the relationship puzzle that comes directly from *The 50 75 100 Solution*.

Do the Math

- Relationships with significant others are often the toughest ones we have, at least in our adult lives. If not, there would be no such thing as breakups or divorce, and marriage counseling would not be as common as it is (though probably not as common as it should be).

- The single most important first step to changing these dynamics is not convincing the other person that they are wrong or that you are right, but instead seeking to understand what they *really* want and focusing on *that* instead of how they are treating or mistreating you. This is an active, conscious, repetitive step you must take.

- Through recognition of what they really want, you will see how you may sometimes stand in the way of it, which insights their actions and reactions, even if you did not intend to do so. And you will see how to interact differently to either not get further in the way or to help get them to the Happiness they seek.

- Because of how these relationships impact us, the ripple effect of the dysfunction (or health) in them touches the rest of our lives. That can make doing the work harder at times, but the value of doing it greater than in most other relationships we face.

- Ultimately, we are going from defensiveness to empathy and compassion. The key is to remember the mission of our relationship in difficult moments, to support each other as we strive to achieve our Happiness.

9.

Parent–Child Relationships

Whether we have kids or not, we all have relationships with children and parents because each of us was a child to someone who was a parent to us.

Even if we grow up orphans and never know our parents, we still have parents, and their existence and relationship to us matters. And, of course, someone else may have played that role for us. Regardless of how our parents earned that title – through biology, law, love, circumstances or otherwise – the relationship between a parent and a child can be both the most beautiful and difficult relationship dynamic many of us faces. The implications of how that relationship plays out can last for decades if not generations.

I want to specifically speak about the two sides of the coin that are at play, and which everyone finds themselves on at least one of, if not both, relationships with our children and relationships with our parents. I have been honored to be able to serve in both capacities, having been a child to two people (and step-child to three others), and as the father of the most amazing boy I could ever hope to help raise.

No matter how good or how close the relationships may be, there are absolutely tough times within them, and some of those tough times last for long stretches where the dynamic needs work to get to a better place.

Some will say that, because of the bond you share with your parents or your children, you will always love each other no matter what and things will always be ok in the end. Because of that, perhaps it does not matter if you do the work, right?

Of course it matters.

I have seen enough cases of families that do not speak to each other, parents whose hearts break for a path their child took that lead to a seemingly-uncrossable divide between them, and people who regret not fixing a broken parent-child relationship after one of the two passes away and they can no longer fix it.

Like any other tough relationship I discuss in this book, the mechanisms used to improve things are the same, so why bother going through yet another set of examples? The parent-child relationship – like that with spouses or other types of significant others – is unique and nuanced enough to warrant dedicated discussion.

As a Parent

Starting from the perspective of a parent, we are treated to the most blatant example of the power of Happiness Seeking in being the catalyst for relationship change when our children are toddlers.

The child-psychologist Dr. Harvey Karp, in his *Happiest Toddler on the Block*[6] series, talks about how frustration with difficulties communicating their desires and emotions leads toddlers to have melt-downs you seemingly cannot stop.

Because young kids who are just grasping the use of language are not always understood, and because their brains have trouble processing information and translating it into coherent external messages as they get more and more

---

[6] http://www.happiestbaby.com

overwhelmed or upset, toddler's ability to be reasoned with essentially shuts off.

He talks about using "caveman speak" to diffuse the situation. You basically get down on their level, make a grumpy face, and say something like, "You're upset. You don't like it. You want the toy!" You speak in short, basic phrases that just aim to validate to their brains that they are understood.

Upon feeling validated, the toddler brain starts to reduce the overwhelming flood of messages it is trying to process as it just focuses on this new stimulus you are giving them that you "get them." The crying (usually) stops, and you can slowly and in basic terms start to talk them through a path forward.

My wife and I saw Dr. Karp talk about the approach, laughed at it, thought it was surely not really going to work but agreed to try it anyway, and were blown away at how effective it was. It was not 100% effective 100% of the time, but it was that effective most of the time, which was better than anything we had to use in its place.

Why is that? Essentially, these toddler brains are not able to bring in all the complexities of an adult mind, so they go to the basics. The one basic desire all of us has is to be happy. Appeal to their Happiness Seeking, and you can see an immediate and complete turnaround.

While this works wonders on toddlers, it works less immediately and simply as we grow older, given the complexities of emotions, responsibilities, different preferences, family dynamics and power struggles and our own confusion over who we are and what we really want play out. Trying to talk like a caveman to a teenager will likely either make them angrier or they will roll their eyes and walk away!

The delivery style needs to change, but the idea being delivered does not. We need to pause our action-reaction cycle to try to see what it is they truly want.

If we feel disobeyed, we may think our child just does not want to listen to us. If they fail at something important at school, we may think they just do not care about their futures. Whatever the situation, when we focus on something self-centered or proximate to the bad behavior, we are missing the point. When our behavior is guided by this misguided focus, we drive a bigger wedge between us and our child.

When your child disobeys you by staying out past curfew, taking your car when they did not have permission, goes out with a friend you do not want them hanging around with or anything else, stop and ask yourself why they are doing this.

If your answer has anything to do with you, it is the wrong answer, it is too surface-level. You need to get deeper.

Why do they want to disobey you? Is it perhaps that they are trying to figure out their lives for themselves, working through their independence, trying to fit into a group they want to be a part of or any other number of possibilities that do not come back to you? And whatever possibilities you arrive at, you need to ask why that matters to them. What might they be going through right now that makes this important?

Another thing to probe is whether they would still have done this thing if you had not told them not to. The answer is almost always, yes. That reaffirms the idea that the Happiness they are seeking is not to disobey mom/dad/whatever role you play.

So what do you do with the answers you start to come up with? You piece them together into a picture of your child's Happiness Seeking. You may not get it right, or you may feel that you cannot understand what they might possibly be trying to achieve that makes any sense to you.

That is ok.

What you will definitely get at the very least is a basis to sit down with them as someone who is not a barrier to their Happiness.

You change your role in relation to what they want, which will allow you to slip in a little closer to them. Had you just gone into their room to yell at them about taking the car or whatever they did, and how they disobeyed you, you would doing the same thing as trying to reason with a screaming, kicking toddler. Instead of melting down more, your older child would just feel like you do not understand them, and the rules they are disobeying are out of sync with what they want so they should either keep disobeying these rules or resent you for setting them more than they already do.

When you sit down from a place of trying to understand their real intention – whether you agree with it or not – you open the door to them seeing you as a partner, a supporter, a guide and someone they can open up to. This is what you want.

Just be careful not to assume their intention and state it as fact. Do not walk in saying something such as, "I know you only broke the rules because you wanted to look cool in front of your friends." You may be wrong in your assumption of what Happiness they are seeking, or they may not be ready to see you in a different light yet.

Guide them to that feeling. Ask them about it. Try to figure out why it matters. Offer possibilities but make no definitive statements about what they wanted or were trying to achieve. Let them own their intentions and feelings and be the ones to define them. All of this allows them to feel greater understanding and validation from you.

As a Child

I could share plenty of personal examples from my experience parenting my son, but they are all fairly benign such as watching TV longer than the time we said he could or turning it on when we told him he could not watch it. He is not yet old enough to present us with the kinds of things I saw as a teenager, young adult or even middle-aged child. So rather than sharing specific examples from my parental relationship with my child, I want to move into the parent-child relationship I have the most experience with and that most of us do as the majority of us spend more years as someone's child than someone's parent.

Growing up, I was generally a good kid, though more of a class clown in elementary school than my parents would have liked. Other than that, I never really did anything seriously bad, did not get in trouble with the law, did not drink, smoke or do drugs and was never caught up with the wrong kids.

However, as I wrote about in *Do a Day*, I did struggle with obesity pretty seriously, which I can imagine upset my parents. I can say plainly that they never recognized the real reason, which was anxiety issues, and actually added to the problem by loading on additional anxiety from the issues they had with my weight. That is, missing the Happiness Seeking I was doing (and needed help with) while applying their own definition of it, they contributed to my increasing weight rather than helping lower it, as I imagine was their actual intention in the situation.

For example, my father, who also struggled with his own weight as a child, gave me a lot of looks of disappointment when I was eating or made stern comments about what and how much I was eating. He was focused on me eating less, and the tools he was employing through his actions and then his reactions to my eating were to present me with negative emotions. I was eating that way because of negative emotions inside of me which he did not know or was not aware of or tuned into, so he was only increasing the reasons for my over-eating by assuming it was just about me making a bad choice.

Perhaps most interestingly, I started to lose weight when I was seventeen, and one of the key decisions I made was to try not to eat in front of my father whenever I could control it. I recognized that there was too much emotion around eating when it happened in front of him, and that stood in the way of me feeling happier about myself, and thus not feeling the need to comfort my pain with food. That is, when I removed myself from the influence of his actions and reactions, I actually achieved what he wanted as I lost one hundred pounds. In essence, my father was unwittingly standing in the way of not just the Happiness I was seeking, but his own through his misunderstanding of the goals at play and how he was blocking them.

With my mother, my weight was less of an issue than our roles as parent and child were. For a variety of reasons, I felt like our roles were reversed in many situations. Despite being the child, I felt responsible for things in my life that I saw my friends' parents being responsible for rather than my friends themselves. When I talk about this in public, I do note that this is not all bad – I am very self-reliant and responsible, which is a good thing. But it also led me to feel like things were not going to be ok *unless I was the one who did them*.

The truth is, my perception of the reality of the situation may have been wrong, at least some of the time or in some situations. This could all have been my interpretation and misperception, which could be based on incomplete knowledge of what was really going on or a misunderstanding of what I saw.

At the same time, my general sense of my needs as a child were that they were in danger of not being met unless I stepped in. This is something I discussed at length in *Do a Day* as the type of anxiety I dealt with after my parents divorced – that things would not be alright.

Regardless of what our roles as parent and child actually were or were not, my *feelings* about them were what I was living with (as we all live with our perceptions of our worlds). It is therefore not a question of whether I was right or wrong, or my mother was doing anything bad or harmful, but simply that my perception at the time was that I needed to step into more adult responsibilities to keep the ship afloat.

In my frustration over a perceived role-reversal with my mother, the one with the misunderstanding of the Happiness goal was me. With any of the things I had to do that seemed like responsibilities I perhaps should not have had, I added a lot of emotion to the equation.

Happiness was never about getting a task done. It was about feeling like things were going to be taken care of and would be ok. Completing any task never actually brought me that ultimate sense of stability; since I always feared some other thing would crop up that I would have to handle, so I ultimately never got to my Happiness. And, actually, when I completed each task, it almost reinforced my concern because I had to be the one to do it, and that was the only reason why things were ok.

That kept me in an action-reaction cycle that lead to lots of misunderstandings and tense moments at home. It also led me to treat my mother in a way that I am sure was not how she wanted her child to treat her, since I saw her in a particular light relative to my sense that many things were perpetually at risk.

For my mother, she would comment about how I do not need to worry about or do something, thinking that would help how I was feeling, but in fact, it probably made it worse because I had a general feeling that things would not get done, so letting any one thing slip would start a landslide (obviously, I was catastrophizing since somehow we were all alive, clothed, fed and sleeping with a roof over our heads despite the majority of the tasks associated with that not falling on my shoulders). She was not getting at what I really cared about.

For me, I focused on *what* she did not do rather than trying to understand *why* she was not doing whatever it was I thought she should do. Perhaps there were other priorities I did not know about that she was attending to, as children and adults often prioritize different things. Maybe her brain did not naturally focus on what my brain did, so she was not even aware of those items while she naturally was thinking of others that I was not aware of.

In essence, I was the same as the parent I talked about earlier that thought their child's goal was to disobey their parent rather than seeking something that disobeying the rule would allow them to achieve.

That made me upset because I kept seeing things as wrong and my views as unheard or ignored, and it meant that our interactions were bound to be difficult because we were missing the Happiness each of us was trying to obtain.

I can think of one particularly bad fight, where we actually did take the time afterward to talk through what we were both intending and why. The fight stemmed from some disagreement we had publicly while visiting a college I was interested in as a high school junior. I do not totally remember how it came about since it was over twenty years ago, but I was probably embarrassed by something she said in front of our campus tour guide, and then acted disappointed with her in a way that a parent might act toward a child who had just disappointed them. In response to my treatment of her, she became upset with me, and the whole thing escalated quickly and intensely.

Regardless of the specifics of how it happened, we were not getting along, and sat in silence for the two-hour drive home only to argue intensely once we got back to our house for at least another hour.

As someone who has always been a bit of a fixer, I wanted the problem to be resolved and the fighting to stop. As a stubborn teen, my idea of "fixed" meant it was my views that were what was accepted, which was not the right way to approach solving things.

I went into her room after we each had an hour or so to cool off to try to tell her why I was so upset with her. I wanted to make her understand why whatever she had done was so bad (again, a role-reversal situation with me as the child having to tell her as the parent why her behavior was unacceptable). She was laying down with a splitting headache, no doubt from the prior hours of pain. The upside of her headache was that it kept either of us from yelling.

With that controlling mechanism in place, I walked into her room, and said, "I want to talk about what happened." I did not say much more than that as part of me knew I needed to let her be the parent if there was any hope of making things better. That was surely one kind of Happiness she sought, for her child to treat her as the parent.

She told me in a stern but quiet voice how I had wronged her. She actually kept it fairly short, though not sweet (it really did not have a chance of being sweet, to be fair). I told her why I was upset, and that I felt like this kept happening between us without ever really fixing the underlying cause, and that was what was really bothering me.

I hit on something important – she was also feeling upset about the pattern and how we were not getting along with some regularity. As a parent, she felt hopeless about fixing it, which only hurt her more. She felt I was being stubborn and treating her in a way she did not deserve because she was the parent and I was the child. Of course, she was right, though I felt it was justified because of how I viewed our roles at the time. And yet, despite thinking I was right in behaving that way because of how I was perceiving the situation, it was not in fact how I wanted things to be.

While we interpreted the behaviors at play in opposite ways, we actually had compatible goals. We wanted less fighting in a relationship that fit the norms for a parent and child. For her, that meant respect in how she was treated and for me that meant stability in the situation so that I did not need to step into adult actions as I so-often felt I did.

I walked out of her room feeling a weight had just been lifted that I could not remember ever being free of before. She, unfortunately, stayed in bed with her head pounding, but perhaps less than it had been a short while before. We had dinner that night, and things were just happier.

I will not say we never had an issue after that, I never felt like I had to step in again, or that my mother never felt like I treated her as if we were in reversed roles of how I should treat her. Whether she remembers what I shared that afternoon and whether it changed any of her thoughts or behaviors, I cannot say. What I can say is that I remembered it, and that glimpse into the Happiness she was seeking gave me some insight into how to avoid days like that again. I understood better about my hand in what was going on and how I could do things differently to help keep from triggering what she would feel is a threat to her Happiness.

Did I implement it all starting then?

No. I was not mature enough. If memory serves, I definitely got better at it and we got better together with less fights and less extreme ones when they happened. Where it really paid dividends is as I matured into adulthood. We have certainly had our ups and downs over the years, as most parent-child relationships do, but I have also found more clarity in how to navigate them or how to handle myself in a way that helps me through things that might have triggered a bigger reaction from me in the past, which would in turn trigger a bigger reaction from her.

More recently, we had a particularly tough phone call about something that fit the old mold of reversed roles and my feeling like something was going to fall apart. She wanted to give us a sapling from a tree my grandfather had planted. It was a very thoughtful and sentimental gift. Despite the sentiment, when she first raised the idea about a month before the phone call, I said that it was not something I could deal with right now, so I could not take the tree. I thought that was the end of it, and did not give it another thought.

Several weeks later, she called to tell me that she had the sapling ready for me to plant. Unfortunately, I had to do a lot of work to receive it as we did not have anywhere around our home I could plant it, and I had only a couple of hours to spare before going to a book signing I was doing.

And because it was November in Massachusetts, I could not really wait as the ground would be frozen any day. While I appreciated the idea, I really was not in a position to deal with it, but also felt trapped as, unfortunately, the sapling had already been uprooted and needed to be replanted.

This kind of situation is one I call a "Last Cookie" situation. If there is only one cookie left, and we both want it, you have to go without your Happiness for me to get mine and *vice versa*. Sure, we could split the cookie, but then we each get less than we really wanted, and in this particular situation, the tree would die if we split it or only half-planted it. My mother wanted to give us the baby tree, and I wanted to not have to deal with it at that time. One of us would have to give up our Happiness for the other to get it.

Because there really was no ability for me to say, no, (whether real or in my mind), I had to stop spending time with my family, change out of the clothes I had put on for my event, go dig up something else in our yard that had been happily living in the little space we have, plant her sapling, and then shower again, get dressed a second time, and hope I get to the book store on time to setup up for my event. And, of course, I did all of this while moaning and groaning about how annoyed I was, and how this was reliving my childhood of having to do things I did not want to do because of actions or inactions of my mother. This particular version of the situation was a common one where I would say, no, to something, and she would act as if I had said, yes, and then try to insist I had never said, no, and was being difficult or mean to her when she was trying to be nice.

After planting the tree and getting ready for my event (again), I called my mother to talk about the situation because I felt it was important for her to understand the impact her decision had on me so we could try to avoid situations like that in the future. I did not want to argue with her, but merely for her to see that there are other Happiness goals that were impacted as she sought hers so she could be more sensitive going forward and perhaps listen to me the first time I had said, no.

Unlike when I was young, I could see what could potentially happen on this call. So I made a choice, proactively, to manage my actions and reactions so that I could give my mother something different to interact with than my historic responses might have otherwise given her. Rather than start the call by attacking her for "doing this to me", I needed to frame this as wanting her to just understand the context that was at play when she gave us the sapling that day. I felt it was important to recognize and respect her desire to be seen as the parent in the situation, which meant that she was trying to do something nice for her child in this instance.

Despite my intentions, the call still got heated. I controlled my tone (or at least I did as far as I could tell), and said what I was hoping to say as I had hoped to say it. Despite that, she still felt like I was trying to say she was a bad person, or had done something mean, so she responded angrily and hurt. I cannot blame her because she would certainly have been justified in those assumptions in the past, and was probably just reacting to what she *thought* was going on under the surface.

That is, she was presuming a Happiness goal on my part that was not there.

Rather than reacting to her tone and words, I stayed the course because that would keep me on the best path to the Happiness I was seeking. My intention was for the impact of her actions on me to be recognized in hopes of being appreciated next time something like this comes up. I did not want her to feel bad – in fact, that was one thing I specifically wanted to avoid (so her not feeling bad was part of my definition of Happiness). That helped me keep from yelling or arguing.

That is so crucial. Parents and children know far too well where each other's buttons are, and often get too lost in past dynamics to keep from pressing those buttons, even if doing so is against the Happiness we seek. That is why we need to keep Happiness Seeking front and center, try to discover what the other person's Happiness truly is, and not just what we *believe* their Happiness to be. That can help save us from giving them something unhelpful to interact with, which will only make things worse through the interconnected nature of our relationships.

With my true goal in mind, I reiterated how I knew her intentions were good, and how what she was doing was such a great thing – sharing something her father created with her kids. We were all so close to him, and of course we all appreciate the gift and the idea behind it. I paused there so she could process my understanding of her intention and really of the Happiness she was seeking – to share a piece of her father with her children and be appreciated for doing so.

Had I said all of that and then reiterated that it was just not a good time for me, I had tried to tell her that repeatedly, but she would not listen and now it has been a burden I was not in a place to deal with, it would basically have invalidated her sense that I "got her".

Unfortunately, while the heat dissipated, the call was still tense, and ended awkwardly. A few minutes later, the phone rang, it was my mother. She was calling to thank me for explaining what I was feeling and to apologize for putting that on me at a bad time. We had a good conversation that focused on her intentions, how nice of a gesture it was, and me sharing a bit more of what was happening on my end that made it bad timing in general, but also why the specific incident was less of my concern than changing the pattern for the future. That was compatible with both of our goals since she could still offer the kind gesture she wanted to offer and feel like she is seen as doing caring things for her children (and acting in the role of parent), and I could also know that she would respect my situation in the future, which would help me feel less angst about things going wrong (which is basically how I felt about needing to scramble to deal with the tree before going to my book signing when I should have been focusing on my event).

Step-Parent / Step-Child

There are other parent-child relationships that can be even more complex, such as step-parent-step-child. I have had step-parents since I was eleven years old, and had parents who had boyfriends or girlfriends since I was much younger. And while I have a step-father, he is not the same step-father I had when I was growing up, so there is a new dynamic of being an adult step-child and new adult step-siblings.

I have not only had my own relationships with my step-parents to experience, but I was aware of my parents now having someone else involved in the parental circle around their kids (and new step-grandparents), new step-siblings to get along with or not, and my step-parents' ex-spouses. It is quite a complex network of relationships, personalities and intentions.

For the immediate step-parent-step-child relationship, of course the tools are the same. Start with Happiness Seeking. Think about the Interconnectedness of the relationship and how changing your behavior in respect of the Happiness they Seek can change the dynamic of the relationship; and maintaining hope through the idea that all things are ultimately Impermanent, even problems in a relationship.

What is different, or more accurately a specific nuance that is common to many of these relationships is around the end of the parents' marriage and how the step-parent may be seen in relation to that. This can be a real perception on the part of the step-child (whether they are aware of it or not), or it can be a wrong assumption on the part of the step-parent who then acts with that presumption in mind and creates a flawed dynamic.

For me, I did not connect the existence of my step-father (before he and my mother got married) as having anything to do with my father. I did not have a desire or hope that my parents would get back together, and see him (or my step-mother, for that matter) as standing in the way. He and I got along, and I liked him. There were moments where we butted heads, though, and this was usually around stylistic differences in parenting from what I was used to, or when he felt I was not treating his own kids well enough.

The last situation is particularly tough. His parental instinct is to protect his children above all else, and here was this "other kid" not being kind enough to them. For me, I was going about my life, living in my house, and now these "other kids" were there, and my mother, who used to dote on me, was doting on them. And we had all sorts of different kinds of things going on. Different music playing in the car (or, actually not music at all but rather a local sports radio station), different brands of food in the fridge, my mom was smoking with someone whereas she had not smoked before, we were living in a different house than we had been, and we would visit our father for the weekend. I did not necessarily actively think about wanting my old life back (it was, after all, one with lots of arguing, which I did not like either), but I felt uncomfortable or perhaps not at home in my home.

If he had presumed any issue I had with him was because he was in the way of my parents getting back to together, anything he said or did around that would not help me feel connected with him. It may not make things worse, but it would not help me feel comfortable with all the changes afoot.

If he told me not to treat his kids badly, he would miss that I was not intending to, but was merely a little kid feeling uncomfortable in his own home and acting out at one of these new things in the home (and imagine how his kids must have felt there!).

If you pick it apart, we actually wanted the same thing. Comfort. He wanted to protect his kids, who were going through a very difficult, confusing, sad experience as their parents split up and they had to be introduced to these new people, a new home to visit, where they did not have their bedrooms, and were subjected to behavior from those other kids that made them feel bad.

What if he had come to me with comfort as the theme? I could understand that. After all, I was the kid who was eating as much as he could to try to get more comfort in his life. And if he appealed to the idea of comfort, he could add to that the perspective his kids were having, and how that is all they really wanted, too. A conversation like that would help me feel different about him and see him as someone who understands what I was going through, *and* feel different about his kids in those moments where I was not treating them the way he wanted me to because I would identify with them.

He never really had that talk with me, but he did make a real effort to try to bring comfort into the equation. Things were generally laid back in the house (sometimes too much so for my sense of things not being taken care of). We did things in the house that were fun (or at least to a kid) like all the kids making dinner together. That also helped us kids bond and naturally see each other as being in the same boat.

While we are not legally step-siblings anymore, I still consider his kids my sisters because of how close we got as we all grew up. That came from a shared desire to be more comfortable in the lives that we had instead of a desire to go back to lives that did not include these new "other kids".

Do the Math

- Parent-child relationships are the only kind that everyone experiences one way or another, officially or unofficially.

- While the tools of making better parent-child relationships are the same as for other relationships, sometimes we struggle in applying them because of how close we are and the history at play in our dynamics. The key is to step back and think about Happiness Seeking by asking probing questions about their Happiness *and* your own.

- The biggest issue with parents and children, regardless of age, is that they do not "get us". This goes for both parents and kids. Setting aside our assumptions to find what really motivates our behavior toward each other is the path to making things better.

- Kids do not generally disobey a parent because they want to disobey and parents do not generally make rules to control their kids. Both sides need to work on understanding the reasons why there are rules and why they get disobeyed to make things work.

- Ultimately, most parents want to feel like good parents and most children want to feel safe, secure and loved. At any age. What makes us feel that way may change.

10.

Work

I mentioned earlier a situation at a prior job where I used *The 50 75 100 Solution* to diffuse a major threat, saving my job and making my company better off in the process.

I want to go deeper into that story so you can see how I used the approach to change the relationship dynamic. I also want to share another example from a different work situation where it was crucial in allowing forward progress to continue. In that example, the relationship issue was between me and my direct manager rather than a peer. That helps illustrate that roles do not actually matter in whether the approach can help or not. The only thing that matters is whether you apply the thinking or not.

Before I talk about either of these situations, I wanted to point out something very different about work relationships from those with significant others, friends or family members.

At work, the Happiness people seek is often much more obvious or at least it is simpler in nature. Feeling safe and secure is a more nebulous notion that people need to truly *feel* at a deep level to satisfy. Getting a promotion or the company making its sales target are discreet, obvious things people may want. Even the broad idea of someone wanting to have power can be made more discreet when you realize promotions, titles, staff and budget size are all forms of power or steps along a path to achieving it.

While these tough work situations can be hard to live with, they can also be far easier to solve than troubles in other relationships. Only here, "solving" may mean moving to an acceptably-better place in the relationship, such as not having the other person constantly trying to get you fired (the "death" of your job). This contrasts with a marriage, where you probably would not be happy if you just were not trying to kill each other anymore.

Co-Workers

I gave a high-level rundown of the first story I want to share with you in *Happiness Seeking*. To refresh your memory rather than asking you to skip back, I had a brilliant and highly-respected coworker who had gone from being a strong ally and support to suddenly and severely turning into someone who seemed hell-bent on taking me down. We had confided in each other, bounced ideas off each other, and supported the major initiatives we both had going on. People periodically commented to me about needing to watch out for her because she can be extremely tough, which I saw, but I do not mind people who are tough if they are also fair and what they are being tough about is good. I had certainly seen cases where she went on the attack, and I did not agree with her style or her position, but we all have times where we make mistakes and act in ways we later regret, so I was not about to pass broad judgment on her based on some of these behaviors.

That is, not until she did it to me. Just like how I talked about viewing a boss who is tough on someone you think deserves it versus tough on your friend leads to you feeling differently about that boss, I suddenly found myself agreeing with those who had warned me about her.

Some major things were happening in the business that had the potential to be quite destructive financially, so obviously the entire subject matter brought with it a lot of fear, discomfort and a healthy dose of disbelief. She took the position of this last feeling, claiming that these negative developments must be wrong, and that I was the one behind them. She sent a scathing email to our boss, and put myself and our Chief Financial Officer on the CC line, talking about how these actions were wrong and then told a story of me going off privately to take the actions without consulting anyone and after the decision-making body who would make the call on these types of moves had already met and not arrived at these conclusions. As a member of that group, she used her position in it as proof that I had not shared the decisions publicly and did them in secret.

She left out a few key facts, however. First, she had not attended any of the group's meetings in the two-or-so-years that I had been there. She just never showed up without even sending her apologies, an explanation or declining the meeting invite. The CFO and I both did attend those meetings, so she was playing a dangerous game by painting a picture of being in the meeting herself.

Second, the timing of the events that lead to the decision came after the meeting due to last minute developments. I did not have the authority to make the kind of decisions that were made, so I had to discuss with my boss what the developments were and how to handle them. He felt strongly that we should do what we ended up doing, and we alerted the rest of the leadership of the company, including the CEO, who I talked to about it at length.

And, lastly, despite her insistence from a position of expertise on the subject that the decisions I made were wrong (and she had done no analysis or review of the facts to determine that, as I could tell she had not logged into the system with the information since before any of this happened), we had in fact verified all of the information and gotten expert opinions on everything. While the news was bad, it was correct. Sometimes, that is just the way things are.

But herein lies the beginning of the root of her Happiness Seeking. She had been responsible for my area in the past, so these developments reflected negatively on her work. She was currently responsible for several things that were feeding into the developments and was not addressing the underlying issues behind them, which was squarely in her new remit. While the company is not one that sets out on witch hunts ever, she – understandably – must have felt threatened or concerned. If she did not feel either of those things, she may just have felt that her intelligence was being threatened, challenged or questioned, which is not something she (or most people) takes well to.

In her defense, she, like the rest of us in the leadership team, wanted the company to thrive. She had invested a lot of herself in the success of the business since the very start of it. She cared deeply about it, and had done a huge amount of good.

This news was rough for the business, and, while we would certainly weather the storm just fine, it was a pock mark on an otherwise impeccable track record in which she correctly felt some ownership. While this was "just a job", when you put so much of yourself into it, it can be hard to separate yourself as a person from the performance of the business. When the business performs poorly, you take it very personally. On top of that, our compensation was closely tied to the business's performance, so this negative development would directly impact all of our earnings. I cannot say whether she cared about that or not, but it would be understandable if she did. And while she may have, I can pretty safely assume that the personal responsibility she felt for the business was probably a bigger input into her reaction than whether she would get paid less.

With that background, I had a choice when she sent her email. It was a Friday evening, so I could not just go and talk to her or the CEO about it. My initial desire was to send an email back refuting all of her points, backing myself up with the verifiable facts I had. I wanted to call the CEO at home and go off about how angry I was to be treated like this and that she would be allowed to behave that way. I wanted to send her an email separately blasting her and her behavior. I wanted to email the CFO and commiserate as I knew he was on my side.

But I did none of that. Instead, I sent an email to everyone, and thanked her.

That's right. I realized that arguing, whether in person or especially via email, was not the path to resolving the matter. And if I blew up, I would look unprofessional and probably just give fuel to the fire around the idea that I did not know what I was doing and could not be trusted with the responsibility I had.

So I sent an email thanking her for her concern and the work she had done to try to understand whether this was perhaps a mistake as that would mean the business would not take a hit. I decided not to debate each of her points, and merely said, "I have information that paints a different picture from the points you made, but we should all get together to discuss this since it is so important. I will find us time on Monday."

Of course, I was not as calm inside as my email made it seem like I was, but I knew I needed to change the interaction if I was going to change the outcome. She is too smart, too well-trained at arguing, and too respected for me to win in a head-to-head battle. So not only did I send that email and find us time to meet, but I also knew I needed to spend some time reflecting on the situation to ensure I was truly calm when I walked into that meeting. The answer, of course, was to reflect on the three Buddhist principles behind *50 75 100* so I could employ the approach in the meeting.

I started with Happiness Seeking. I outlined above the various reasons she was likely doing what she was doing. Each of these points of anger or frustration for her relate to something she wants – to see the business unscathed and thriving. The thing about that definition of Happiness is that it is what I want, too. Knowing that immediately impacted my mood as we were not dealing with a situation of conflicting interests. We were not both trying to eat the last cookie here. Instead, we wanted the same thing for the business, and she perceived that I did not or that I was working against that outcome.

That means my job in the meeting would not be to argue with her about why she is wrong. Going toe-to-toe, as I said, would not be a guaranteed way to get through this with her. Instead, my job would be to show her that I am aligned with her on the outcome and can help us get there rather than being the perceived blocker or threat to it that she thinks I am. That leads to a totally different set of behaviors and approaches on my part.

Next, I had to help myself reset from my reactive state. Seeing that we had aligned definitions of Happiness helped, but I had to remember that she had once seen me very positively. She had been the most welcoming to me of all of our peers when I joined the company. She had been so supportive along the way. We shared a lot of personal interests and values outside of work. That is, there is proof that our Interdependent definition of each other can be good. That actually goes beyond just hope that it could become good, but a verifiable fact that it generally has been.

Without doubt, our views of each other were certainly off course. Given that they had been good, I focused on the idea that everything changes, so there is no reason to assume it will now be constantly in a bad place, just as our relationship had not stayed constantly in a good place. It can change.

Just being aware of these things is helpful. It frames the mind in the right way to move forward. However, that is not necessarily enough, especially not early on when one is trying to follow *The 50 75 100 Solution* in really heated situations, as this was sure to be. So I gave myself some structure and tools to keep me on course. I typed up a goal for the meeting, which focused on the outcome of protecting the business so it can flourish. That would directly appeal to her definition of Happiness. Then I went through her various points, and put together the countering facts I had, but then I wrote out responses that did not focus on a, "No, you are wrong. It isn't X, it's Y," approach, but rather focused on the goal of the impact on the business.

I shifted my points away from being responses trying to dismiss or disprove her points, which would only serve to make her feel attacked back, misunderstood or like she is dealing with someone too stupid to understand what is going on. I shifted them to being statements that brought clarity to an emotional discussion which would help move it toward seeing how to protect the business and recover. I reviewed everything several times, including my read on the three Buddhist principles in this situation, my sense of the goal of the meeting and my notes on the points I wanted to share.

When we walked into the meeting, it started as I expected it would – heated. I opened by thanking everyone, and especially her for pointing out the concerns about what had happened. I shared my goal for the meeting to try to set the tone.

Then it began.

She launched into a bit of a tirade, reiterating the points she sent in her email, citing people and data to prove that I was wrong and the way I had handled things was flawed. I just sat there and let her speak. I did not try to respond, interrupt or show through body language that I was stifling doing any of those things. I just let her speak.

When she was done, I thanked her again. I acknowledged how serious the issue was and that she was right to raise her concerns. Then I brought up the goal of the meeting again to reframe our intention to help the business. I asked her what her goal was. I asked her what she wanted. What I was doing was asking her to define her Happiness.

That completely disarmed her. She visibly let go of at least part of her anger, with her shoulders dropped and her posture relaxing. You could literally see it happen. See, if she saw me as a blocker to her Happiness, suddenly I had shown myself not to be and that I was actually turning to the side to allow her Happiness to come through. I may not yet be an ally in her mind, but I was clearly not a threat. That let her back off a bit.

She answered the question more or less as I expected her to, essentially saying how she was concerned about the impact on the business and that it may not be something we could recover from. She did not say anything about me being wrong, needing to be fired or anything of the sort. She did bring up the compensation impact, but not for her so much as the impact on everyone's compensation.

I thanked her. Only I did not stop there, I validated her position, agreed with it, and stated my concern as the same. I referred back to my comments when we started the meeting about what I was hoping we would achieve as a sign that I, too, want the same thing and that is what I am hoping to take out of this meeting. That was the point where she not only saw me no longer being a blocker to her Happiness, but actually being someone who would try to help achieve it.

So with our dynamic shifted, I went over the points I wanted to share, not as a rebuttal to her, but as a way to bring the group up to speed on where we really were. The CFO chimed in several times to support what I was saying or offer more clarity or information to strengthen the points I was making.

We ended up agreeing that, in fact, the bad news was not fake news, unfortunately. But we also saw several things we could do to manage how it impacted the business and what we could do going forward to undo some of the impact it would still have.

While my relationship with that coworker was never what it had been before, it also was never what it was around this incident again. She clearly no longer liked me, and I would hear from people about disparaging comments she would make about me (and others) when we were not around. But we could work together and we could move the business forward. That is all that I really wanted. We did not have to be friends, but we did have to collaborate for the betterment of the business, which is the Happiness we both were seeking.

Your Boss

At a prior company, before I had even discovered *The 50 75 100 Solution*, I had a manager who was by far the worst boss and leader I have ever had. That is partially because I have gotten to work for some great people, but I have also, unfortunately, worked for some deceptive or inept (or deceptive and inept) people.

My boss in this other role had been at the company since its founding several decades earlier, and had worked her way up from an administrative role to the C-suite. She was a role model in some respects, but she was also universally feared and avoided because of her incredibly political, suspicious, duplicitous nature.

When I interviewed with the company, I thought she was great and was very impressed by her and excited to get to work with her. When I got the job offer, I saw that I would be reporting to her instead of the CEO, as I had originally been told I would be. I mentioned that to a friend who had connected me with the opportunity originally, and he said I had to turn down the offer immediately and that I could never work for her.

I thought that was so strange since she seemed so great. He told me several clear examples of what I would come to find out she was like, and suggested I go meet with the CEO about it.

I did just that, talking with him about the role and mentioning my surprise on the reporting line change from what we had discussed. He explained why he had done that, which made sense, but then he went on to caution me about working for her. He outlined all of the same concerns my friend had stated.

I was puzzled why the CEO – her boss – would allow her to behave this way or would keep her around, which he shared with me without me even saying anything. I did not agree with his reasoning as I always think it is better to remove someone damaging to an organization rather than use them for something (like having a 'bad guy' to do your dirty work to keep your nose clean since everyone dislikes that person anyway) or if you think the pain of their exit and the loss of whatever good they do is too much to deal with. He then told me she had privately told him she was retiring within the next couple of months, so I would just need to keep my head down until she left.

It was a very strange situation, but I understood what he was saying, and the offer was good, so I took it. I told my friend about the meeting, and he told me to make sure I really did keep my head down or my life would be miserable.

To make a long story short, my friend was wrong. Not directionally, but she was so much worse than he ever realized. She had a few people she trusted to act as spies or to plant information to see if it got back to her. She would test whether you were loyal to her or to someone else since, if you came to her with this "secret" information you were not supposed to share, then she could trust you. Or she would ask you about things you would have no reason to know that she should know just to see if someone else had told you something she told them not to share.

I always felt so awkward in those situations because she should know exactly what she's asking me for information on, and knows I would not know anything about it, so I always wondered if she was confused or actually knew nothing about her organization. Turns out, she was doing it all intentionally, but perhaps had not realized it made her look ignorant or even perhaps like she was slipping mentally.

The thing that bothered me most was probably how she insisted I tell her everything I would say in our biweekly executive round table meetings. If I did not have her pre-approval on a point, I was not to raise it. That might be ok with things I would present, but it became very problematic whenever people would ask me about something since she likely had not pre-approved for me to speak about it. Rather than sitting there silently or claiming to be clueless, I would answer them. And then I would feel her wrath later for how I was insubordinate for having the audacity to tell people things she did not give me approval to speak about.

It was exhausting. And worse than that, it was costing the organization because we were spending so much effort dealing with her games rather than moving forward on the opportunities at hand. And worse than that, she went to the CEO two weeks after I joined to tell him she had changed her mind and would be staying after all.

The only positive in all of this is that she was not very good at all of this plotting and scheming. She was too obvious, or at least to me she was. You could see it coming from a mile away, and could usually pretty easily play the game to get the outcome you needed, or at least to get her to leave you alone.

Once I realized that, I decided to just play along to avoid her making my life worse (which was not my definition of Happiness). I realized that she was operating from a place of severe insecurity. I wanted to understand where it came from, so I appealed to her desire to be seen as an expert, and asked if she would be open to spending some time with me to tell me a bit more about the evolution of the organization.

In recounting the story, I heard several interesting things about how she viewed peers, direct reports and leaders. The kinds of things she saw as negative or bad performance indicators all revolved around whether she got blamed for something or looked bad. If she made a mistake, that only mattered if someone pointed it out, and the problem in that situation was the person who did the pointing. They were the one who had made a mistake or was flawed somehow. She always seemed to miss that the issue – the performance of the business being harmed – was her doing. Reputation and perception were all that mattered, and she did not seem to appreciate that you can build a great reputation and perception of yourself by performing well and being good to people.

The thing is, she was quite smart, experienced and capable. She just routinely threw that away by trying to manipulate her way through problems. And it had worked beautifully for her throughout her career as she continued to move up the ranks into one of the top positions.

Recognizing what she really cares about is how I was able to survive. Understanding this allowed me to know how to act whenever I was presented with one of her games of manipulation. I did not like it, but I chose to act in a way that reduced the conflict, which meant she would leave me alone for a little while so I could do real work. In the context of the job, that was the Happiness I sought.

While it may feel contrary to your values or like you are approving of your boss being a bad boss, that is simply a question of looking at it the wrong way. You are looking at it out of sync with your own Happiness. If you ultimately want to do a good job (and have the benefits that come with it, whether that is for you, your company, your peers, your customers, etc.), then finding a way to work *with* your boss instead of despite them will get you there.

Leadership expert Jocko Willink wrote about doing exactly this in a piece he wrote for CNBC[7] on how to deal with three kinds of bad bosses: micromanagers, egomaniacs and detached bosses. In none of these scenarios does he talk about trying to break or change them, get them fired or work around them. He talks about how to recognize what

---

[7]Available at http://www.5075100.com/jocko

motivates them and working with that motivation as you go about achieving your goals.

As for me, I ultimately left the company because I had other opportunities that would not suffer from such silliness. In hindsight, while there were many painful moments, I got some hilarious stories to share about all the things she would do and do not harbor any bad feelings because I understand and appreciate the underlying dynamics at play on her end.

Unfortunately, though, I left behind some amazing people in my teams, who still had to deal with her for a little while. She generally left them alone as she deemed them too junior to be worth her attention, but I did worry about no longer being able to be a buffer for them. I heard from a friend there that she ended up retiring eventually, so the good people of the company can finally do the amazing work they are all capable of without having to worry about playing any games.

These two examples show that you can bring the three core principles from Buddhism into tough work situations, whether that is with a peer, a boss or anyone else. Doing so starts you on a path to understand how you might be able to change your approach to them to result in a different outcome. It may not make everything perfect, but if it brings you closer to your definition of Happiness, then it is a win.

Do the Math

- Like any other relationship, the start of solving tough work relationships begins with Happiness Seeking – understanding what the other party wants, what you want, and how the two can coexist.

- Unlike many closer relationships, those at work may be more about coexistence than moving to true happiness. We do not need the other person to love us or be our best friend at work like we do in our home life.

- While the dysfunctions we face at work may be tougher in some respects, and the consequences may seem worse (losing your job means losing your ability to pay your rent or mortgage, buy food for your family, etc.), the path to fixing them or getting them to a sufficiently-better position may be easier because, often, the definitions of are more discreet and explicit than with loved-ones.

11.

Life

As we go out into the world and deal with people, we have all sorts of relationships that could benefit from *The 50 75 100 Solution* beyond just those I discussed already.

The way you deal with these other relationships is the same, while the specifics of how you apply them will differ based on the nuances of each situation. In some cases, these interactions will be the "once and done" variety where you never deal with that person again, like my example of getting cut off on the highway. In others, we will have ongoing opportunities to learn what the other person really wants, how to interact with them in a way that positions us in line with their Happiness rather than being perceived as against it, and create a more productive dynamic for both sides of the equation.

Here are a few situations you may face, and how to think about bringing *The 50 75 100 Solution* into them immediately.

Buying a Car *(or Other Big-Ticket Negotiations)*
I was a car salesman (briefly) in the late-1990s. While I may not have sold a ton of cars, I did learn a lot about the process and what pressures the sales staff work with every day, which many buyers may be unaware of that influence the sales person's behavior in the interaction.

This has served me tremendously every time I have bought a car, which many people view as a painful experience. In reality, this situation can apply to other big-ticket purchases or negotiations you may face, such as real estate transactions.

Why is it painful for us?

Simple – we want to get the car we want, equipped as we want it equipped, for as low a price as possible in as little time as we can take doing it. And we do not want to feel like we have been taken advantage of or were dealing with an adversary we cannot trust (or stand), though we often expect that to be an inevitable part of the process.

That pretext of expecting a difficult and adversarial experience influences our actions and reactions, of course, which contributes to having an adversarial and difficult interaction with the dealership at times. So what can we do about it?

First, we need to start by trying to understand the Happiness the sales person seeks. There are many factors that go into their definition of Happiness, some of which you may expect and some you may not even realize exist. Car sales people have quotas they have to meet, which can mean their job is constantly in jeopardy (if they miss their numbers, they could be fired). That, in turn, means their ability to pay their bills is at risk (since they are paid a commission on each sale), and every minute they are not closing a sale takes away from their job security and potential earnings.

That last part is crucial.

If they do not see you as a serious buyer, you are not just wasting their time but putting them in financial danger. That means that, while you may have seen them as the aggressor or the bad one in the interaction, they may see you in the same vein. And, of course, you not getting your way with them just means you do not get the car you want, you pay more than you planned (or walk away if it is too much more), or it takes more time than you wanted it to. For them, you being bad means they may lose their job, their home, their ability to buy food for their children, etc. The stakes are higher for them in most cases than they are for you.

Most of us do not see it this way, and certainly most of us do not intend to put anyone's financial well-being at risk. But understanding this is very helpful in framing our behavior, which will ultimately increase the likelihood that we get what we want in the end. And most of us would agree that getting what we want without hurting the other person or putting them in danger of losing their livelihood is a good thing

One way to start the interaction on a markedly better note is to come into the dealership knowing what you want. This used to be hard since we had limited access to information, so you really had no choice but to learn through visiting a dealership. Nowadays, you can do lots of research on the models, features, competitors, pricing, etc. You can get the exact cost the dealer pays for the car, how much they mark it up, any rebates or incentives offered to you by the manufacturer and even special kick-backs the dealer may be getting. You can design the exact car you want, check inventory at various dealerships and even pre-negotiate before you ever set foot in a showroom. That means that when you do finally come in and take a sales person's time, it is to do a deal (if one can be made). Let them know that you are clear on what you are looking for and can make a decision that day as soon as you start your interaction with the sales person.

I have started my car purchasing discussions by letting them know I have looked into the car, I tell them the configuration I want with specific items named using the manufacturer's specific names such as their name for the color you like (which is a signal to them that you really do know what you want; for example, do not just say, "Blue," but rather, "Elektra Blue".), and exactly where I am in the process. Contrary to what some people may tell you, transparency around this does not remove any of your bargaining chips, but rather takes out any sense on the sales person's part that they have to play a game with you to sniff out what is really going on.

I would generally say something like, "I am interested in this model in this color with this package, I would love to see the one you have in stock, and if the numbers are good, we can do a deal today." More specifically, when I negotiated for a Ford Escape a few years ago, I told the salesman after the normal greetings, "So I am looking at getting 2014 Escape Titanium in Magnetic Gray with the tow hitch package. I see you have one in stock, so I would love to check it out. And if the numbers work out, we could do this deal today."

As backup, in my pocket, I had a print out of the inventory page for that exact car, as well as a page from a website that lists the invoice and retail pricing involved, broken down by option. It turned out I did not need any of that information because I had set the stage clearly within the first few minutes.

By putting my cards on the table, my actions lead to the sales person and his manager reacting by putting theirs on the table, too. And if they did not, then I would get an early signal that they are not the kind of people I want to work with, so I could simply take my business elsewhere without wasting too much time. That is, if it worked toward me getting the car at a good price quickly, then my Happiness was going to be reached. If it did not work out, then at least it would not take away from my Happiness because I would quickly be able to move on to another dealership.

What I have found by using this approach is that I am able to close a deal in a single visit and in a short amount of time. I have also walked away with a deal I feel very good about because I not only got what I was hoping to in terms of product and price, but I also felt comfortable with the level of transparency on the dealer's part that I was not secretly being taken advantage of.

For a sales person to be able to close a deal within ninety minutes, including a test drive, is very fast. If they can see that as a high likelihood from the initial interaction because of your openness and pre-work, you will change their behavior pre-emptively.

That includes something very important that many people do not think about. In most car dealerships, sales people do not have pricing authority. Instead, they go back to a sales manager to get a price, and act as your representative in their discussion with the manager, who is obviously putting the dealership's finances above yours. The reality is, while the sales person represents you, their interests are more closely aligned to the dealership, yet they know they need to at least bring you something good enough to keep you from leaving. It is a tricky dance for them.

When you show them from the start of the interaction that you know what you want and are prepared to move quickly, you help sway them to advocating for you with their managers more than they would otherwise because they see the value in doing so (and all of this may be happening subconsciously for them). Having someone who knows you are serious and who recognizes that you are supportive of their Happiness, rather than someone putting it at risk means they will push their manager harder because they will feel closer to the finish line by siding with you rather than playing any of the games or tactics their manager may be used to employing. And you will walk away happier, which only means you will like your car that much more.

This is a similar dynamic to buying a home, where the realtor does not accept or reject your price offer, but rather they represent it to the seller and either advocate for or against you. The more they see working with you as a clear path to earning their commission, the more likely they will represent your bid favorably.

Getting Pulled Over

I will admit that I have been pulled over for speeding. It has not happened often, but it has happened more than once. What I learned about changing tough interactions like these has led to smaller fines or simply getting a warning when a full ticket would have been warranted.

The reason is that I recognized what Happiness the officer was likely seeking, and tried to act from a place of facilitating it rather than working against it.

Like the car sales situation, the officer may have a quota (officially or unofficially). They also likely have a desire to stay safe, without getting into the heated issue of whether that fear is founded or not. They may have a desire to be seen as an authority figure and to be respected as such. Additionally, they may have an expectation that the interaction will be difficult and may simply not want to deal with the aggravation at that moment (just as you probably are feeling in those situations).

Given their line of work, we should also remember that there is a framing context at play. They may have just dealt with a difficult situation as part of their job, including potentially having recently put their life on the line for public safety. You, or the situation you are in, may also remind them of a prior challenge to their Happiness. Perhaps it is a poorly lit street, late at night, and the last time they pulled someone over in such a setting, that person attempted something bad such as trying to run the officer over or drawing a weapon on them. While you simply reminding them or something dangerous may not be a justifiable validation for any mistreatment you may suffer, it may explain an unconscious bias on their part that could be guiding their behavior.

Needless to say, there is a *lot* at play in these interactions that is complicated and perhaps not totally apparent to the officer, let alone you. And while I share an example of getting pulled over, this can extend to a broader context of dealing with someone with an official authority over you that may have some very complicated factors at play, such as perceived threats to their safety or the safety of others that you may pose in their mind regardless of whether you pose it in reality.

With that understanding, I have realized that there is basically only one path to not being seen as working against any of these types of Happiness the officer may be seeking – complete compliance and cordiality.

If you feel they are in the wrong and want to push back and challenge them or their actions, or perhaps you feel the need to fight for your rights, the safest place to do that is after the event has concluded through more public, official channels, where someone with a firearm and more authority than you is not in charge, such as talking an attorney and pursuing the matter in court or through a formal complaint.

For me, by understanding what I believe their Happiness to be and how I may appear to be blocking it, I have chosen my actions and reactions carefully, regardless of what they do. I have generally kept my hands visible by placing them on the wheel, opened my window before they came up to the car so they did not have to bang on the window or tell me to do something, addressed them as, "Officer," "Sir," or, "Ma'am," and refrained from giving any commentary or challenge. I have made a point of staying calm and controlled regardless of their tone. That is, I am putting out actions that signal my compliance with their Happiness consistently regardless of any actions or reactions on their part.

The last time I was pulled over, the officer, a New York State Trooper, thanked me for not arguing or being mad at her for pulling me over. She actually had already concluded the interaction, but turned around to come back to thank me as she seemed somewhat in disbelief about it – like she had to wait to be sure I did not shout something at her as she walked away.

I was certainly not happy about getting pulled over (it directly worked against my Happiness, which included getting home quickly and not paying a big speeding ticket or the resultant increases in my insurance premium), but I recognized that *she* was not getting in the way of my Happiness. *I* was with my initial action of driving too fast.

I was speeding. That is not her fault. When I removed the sense that she had done something to me, I could see her as being aligned to my Happiness around the aspect of me not wanting to get a home too late by reminding me that I was acting in a way that put my Happiness at risk (you get home pretty late when you get in an accident from excessive speed, if you get home at all). And having worked in insurance for twenty years, I know that my premium would increase more from an accident than from a speeding ticket, so she was also helping minimize that risk.

My kindness to her resulted in a lower fine than I could have gotten, which meant I paid less than I should have and my insurance was not triggered to increase because of her decisions, which meant she was helping me on my quest for Happiness even more.

If I was angry with her and behaved accordingly, I would have missed all that understanding and surely behaved in a way that increased my fine, or perhaps landed me in the back of her cruiser on the way to a police station.

Now I know not every interaction with the police goes so smoothly, the circumstances may be much more difficult, and the way I look may not result in the kind of reaction the way someone else looks might. I also know that I have friends who are police officers who treat others calmly and kindly even when things are heated or the person they are dealing with is genuinely dangerous.

A close friend of mine, who was a SWAT commander, had a history of not just breaking down doors and storming buildings because he tried to understand the other person and work through the issue toward a peaceful resolution (by negotiating their surrender, which you can generally only do if you try to understand what they want). That approach was better for everyone's Happiness, from the criminal, any hostages, innocent bystanders and the officers who would live through the ordeal; to the police chief, mayor, governor, or anyone else who would not have a major incident on their hands.

Whether you are facing a minor traffic violation or something more serious where my friend may be on the other side of the door with a team of officers with powerful firearms and a battering ram, or if you are appearing in front of a judge, mediator, arbitrator or someone else who can decide or impact your fate, the choices you make about your actions and reactions can dictate how the relationship plays out.

Adult Siblings

When I asked people on social media what relationships they most wanted to hear about in this chapter, the top response was to hear how *The 50 75 100 Solution* plays out in sibling relationships, and specifically those amongst adult siblings. This is a subject I have been studying for over twenty years with deep field research (meaning I am and have adult siblings).

It is very interesting how our sibling relationships change as we go off into our own lives, grow past our childhood dynamics (or do not), or key influences in our relationships (like our parents) are removed from or reduced in the equation. That can make adult sibling relationships unique from their childhood versions in many cases. It is similar to what happens with a caterpillar becoming a butterfly. It is still the same living thing, but it has taken on a totally new look with a new dynamic (though some may say their sibling relationships go from being a butterfly in childhood to a caterpillar in adulthood).

While we still start from the same place of identifying the Happiness our siblings seek when trying to work on these relationships, we have an added lens of our shared past. How is the way we treated each other shaping the way we currently treat each other, or what we want in relation to each other today? Some siblings spend years tormenting each other, then the tormenter grows up and changes, but the one tormented is still left with the pain of the past behavior. Sometimes the torment continues, though perhaps in very different ways. In other cases, the role of tormentor and victim can be swapped.

"Torment" may be the wrong word or at least too strong of a descriptor in other situations. Perhaps one sibling was poorly behaved or would be described as a, "space cadet." Yet as an adult, they may have a master's degree, be a parent, and be a highly successful professional. With their transformation from seemingly aloof and detached to being engaged and successful, how do their siblings see them and consequently treat them? Do siblings come from a place of recognizing that change, or do they still treat the adult as they did the child?

What makes all of these situations harder is the combination of closeness and the time spent building expectations of behavior. It is not dissimilar to difficult parent/child relationships when the child becomes an adult, or many spousal relationships. Even when we have changed, there are norms and expectations at play that can take a long time to overcome.

Yet they can be overcome.

What is important in adult sibling relationships in addition to the basic ideas of understanding the Happiness each of you is seeking in relation to the other, how your actions and reactions are influencing those of the other, and whether you are respecting the capacity we all have to change is that these norms are almost a third party in the relationship that need to be worked on.

The question is, "How?"

For example, one sibling may have been a mean brother due to pain he was feeling from some trauma he experienced. As an adult who has now dealt with the trauma, he has now grown into a compassionate person. The other sibling may have grown up with an established norm of being the object of the brother's anger, receiving a daily dose of verbal and perhaps physical abuse and beratement. That sibling, perhaps a meek and obese younger sister, has now lost weight, become a powerful athlete and successful professional who has found her voice and holds a lot of resentment and anger toward her bother.

For the brother, he wanted to stop hurting as a child, but did not understand his feelings or what to do about them, and likely did not have the help and support he needed for that to happen (or was not open to what he had at his disposal). For the sister in her childhood, she, too, wanted the pain from being mistreated by her brother to stop, and perhaps also holds resentment for those around them growing up for not stopping him.

Today, that sister may want her brother to pay for his abusive past, and may feel that she is the one to teach him a lesson, which is what she thinks she desires more than anything. At a deeper level, her definition of Happy may actually be about not hurting anymore or carrying today's manifestations of yesterday's trauma. She may think that her brother being punished will get her what she ultimately wants, but it likely will not deliver on the healing she seeks despite any short-term benefit to her.

Her brother may feel great shame for how he treated his sister and may be proud of who she became despite his actions. He may want her to know how he feels, but is afraid of addressing the painful past and disrupting the toleration-style coexistence they have moved into. And perhaps that fear he carries manifests itself as awkwardness, distance or other behaviors that appear to come from bad intentions rather than good ones – especially when we remember that he started his journey from a place of pain.

These are difficult and intertwined dynamics that grew over perhaps decades of reinforcing experiences.

Ultimately, each sibling wants their feelings to be known and understood by the other. Each sibling may completely misunderstand the current thinking of the other, and has historically-built expectations of what will happen if they try to talk about their feelings. As a result, they act and react from this place of confused insecurity and pain.

Assuming your safety and the kinds of issues I mentioned before such as addiction and mental health are not issues, there is a path forward through *The 50 75 100 Solution*. Like the transparency in approaching a car purchase, it is important to be transparent in these situations.

Whether you are the brother or the sister in this example, you need to raise the issue. Doing it privately, perhaps in a different setting to physically detach from the established norms even further can help. And try to do it as free from anger, pain or judgment as possible. The key is to remain aware of the risk of agitating the interaction, and avoiding doing so through calmness and patience. It is very similar to what I had to do in that meeting where my coworker was trying to get me fired.

Meeting somewhere privately to talk about the current relationship and trying to make it better is a start. First, acknowledge that the relationship is not what either of you likely wants it to be, and you want it to be better, together.

Then, like a parent trying to understand their teen's Happiness, ask about the definition of Happiness that your sibling seeks. You can get to this with questions such as, "What would be your vision for our relationship?" Or, "If you agree that we are not where we could be, what do you think are the biggest things we should try to work on together?" Do not compare their thoughts to your own as better or worse, but simply focus on understanding what your adult sibling seeks. I find a helpful thing to do is note any points to which you strongly agree with a little comment like, "Oh, me too!" This provides them with validation along the way.

Some of what they say may seem disingenuous or impossible to you given the definition of them that you have built up over the years. It is important to suspend judgment and disbelief because you may not know the current version of them the way you think you do, so your judgment may be of the norms in the relationship rather than the current person you are interacting with.

Once you know what they really want, think about what you want. Can the two coexist? Are they actually the same, even if they are perhaps framed or phrased differently?

What if they seem to sit opposing each other? Think about what you want in relation to them, what they want in relation to you, and then ask yourself why you may want such contradictory things.

What we tend to discover is that seemingly-opposed desires may, at their core, come from a shared goal. Remember the point above about the sister wanting her brother punished, but deeper down, it was really about finally being healed from his past behavior's impact on her?

If your two definitions of Happiness seem to be at odds, it could simply be that you are operating at a surface level rather than the real underlying definition of Happiness.

Talk about it. Be willing to be vulnerable and honest, even if it is scary or hard. The one thing to watch for is whether you are having a conversation with the two of you, or a conversation between two norm-based versions of each other from the past. Be on the lookout for this, and call it out.

That does not mean past hurt is not valid or you cannot say that it mattered to you. It just means that you have to watch for the norm you are focused on and your sibling's currently-stated definition of Happiness being different and whether you are having trouble believing that. If you cannot believe it, you cannot move forward because you will continue to act and react in relation to your expectations regardless of what your sibling does or does not do. The same goes for them.

If this disbelief is too strong, you can find it hard to make any progress, at least for a while. This can change (remember, everything ultimately does), but it can take time. If the expectations are too strong for one of you to move past but the other one is willing to, as long as new actions and reactions are coming from one of you who wants to change the dynamic, the wall can come down for the other. Just as your relationship took years to get to the difficult place it is, it will likely take more than one conversation to change. And that is OK.

One incarnation of this dynamic used to exist between me and my oldest sister. We are nearly ten years apart, grew up in very different situations (she was an only-child (briefly) of two twenty-somethings early in their marriage and spent her elementary-school years as one of two kids. I was the youngest of four born to thirty-somethings who soon got divorced; etc.), and always got along but were very separate due to our age gap.

She often took care of me and my other sister when we were little, almost acting like a cool, young mother who made us cookies and toaster-oven-pizza, drove us places, and then went off to college while I was still in elementary school and had her own apartment in the city soon after that. I was a college kid when she was a mother living in the suburbs.

We remained generationally separated, and that dynamic just kept being reinforced as she was always a milestone or two ahead of me in life. To me, she was this older, mature, cool woman. To her, I was this young boy (though hopefully she thought I was cool, too). While it worked well and we got along great, we had fairly well-defined roles in relation to each other.

As adults, the dynamic continued with us getting along well and even living in the same town. I always held her in high regard as a parent and a person, and still do. As far as I know, she seems to see me similarly. However, on occasion in the past, there were situations where she would speak down to me as if I was her child despite me being an adult. This generally came out in situations involving our parents or our family collectively. It was not a frequent thing, and generally not too heated or intense, but there were a few occasions where it was more pronounced or problematic.

Sometimes it did not matter enough to even bring up, but other times it seemed to get in the way of my Happiness, which would be partially about the reason we were disagreeing but also about being seen as an adult in adult situations. One particular situation went on for several days and got pretty heated. Whatever it was about is not consequential, but it was serious to both of us back then, and we were at a real impasse. We either would not speak or could only seem to argue when we did, which was very different for us.

I think we both realized we would never see eye to eye on the issue, so that piece of each of our sense of Happiness really could not co-exist. The rest of the Happiness we each sought was around our relationship, and that could co-exist, but only with work.

On my commute home from work one night, I called her to talk about the issue in the dynamic without getting into the cause of the arguing. That is, I called her to talk about Happiness Seeking.

I opened by saying I know we think about the situation very differently, and so we want very different things. Neither of us was an actor in the problem, so whether we agreed or disagreed did not mean the outcome would be one way or the other. I said what I wanted to talk about was how hard it had become for us to interact and what we can do about it.

She shared her view of the problem, which was an insight into what she wanted in the relationship. While some aspects of what she said may not have fit with how I read the situation, the bigger picture of Happiness did – for us to stop having this argument. She seemed to want to just say we have to agree to disagree and move on, whereas for me, it was not so much about the content of the argument than the norm at play behind it. We could disagree about the argument, but that was not what I cared about ultimately since sibling arguments end but being sibling does not. We would still be family regardless of how well or poorly we got along.

What I felt was standing in the way of us being OK again from my end was what felt like her dismissing my views or insights into the problem we disagreed about as you might dismiss those of an uninformed child.

My reaction was to feel belittled and invalidated. She did not realize that, and of course the Happiness she was seeking did not include me feeling that way. Part of my reactions so far in this argument came from feeling like she *did* intend this. My feeling intentionality behind her behavior, made it hurt more. When I hurt more, I interacted in less helpful ways, which of course impacted how she interacted with me as we are Interconnected. She had no intention of making me feel this way, so me giving up any insistence that she meant to hurt me allowed me to cool down and stop being as unproductive in our relationship. This, in turn, allowed her to do the same.

It is possible she thought that was an absurd way for me to feel, or that she thought I needed to grow up, toughen up, or that this was my insecurity (probably correct of her) more than *her* issue. However, because we had spent time on the shared Happiness of getting our relationship out of this impasse, she saw the alignment in our goals and was open to hearing me in a way that she would not have if I just called and said, "You are doing these things to me, they are wrong and you need to stop."

I do not think many people would act or react well when presented with that type of comment from another person, yet it is often how we go about these kinds of interactions when we do not stop to think through the three core ideas of Happiness Seeking, Interconnectedness and Impermanence.

Interestingly enough, after we talked about this, and she saw that I actually do have valid, well-developed views of the issue and should not be dismissed while the 'real adults' deal with it, she shifted her thinking on the core issue. She saw why I was concerned about it, and why we needed to work together to try to influence a different outcome than was naturally occurring. I do not think she necessarily saw things my way, which is fine. She did, however, see the risks I was worried about and agreed that we needed to avoid those problems, which we could not do if we were not working together (along with our other two siblings).

The issue in our relationship was really about past norms being too alive and well and dictating our interaction. The impact these norms had was hurt on my part and keeping her from the valuable insights she ended up taking on board and appreciating. For her, it also meant I was behaving in a way that was consistent with the view of me being immature and inexperienced (I was just reacting or lashing out, as a cranky child might). Of course, this influence from these historically-developed behaviors lead us to have a serious problem in our relationship that seemed unsolvable until we called out the root cause.

Bringing It Together

Regardless of the role you play, who you are in the relationship with, whether it is a new or old relationship, or whether this is the last time you will interact or part of an ongoing dynamic, we can approach these situations in the same way to make them more harmonious, productive and happy.

We start by understanding what Happiness is being sought by both sides of the relationship. Understanding this reduces our feelings of being wronged or attacked – at least intentionally or as the sole purpose. This helps to disarm us and our reactions. It also helps us to see avenues to making things better by showing us points to focus on that we think the other person would naturally align to because it fits in with their goals.

Then, by recognizing how we are all Interdependent with each other, we can start to change how the other person is interacting with us by giving them different ideas to interact with through changes in our actions and reactions. While we change our half of the equation, it brings about a change in their half. Sometimes, this can be instantaneous and sometimes it can take repeated effort over days, months or even years.

Because all things in the world change, including relationships, that effort is worth it. Whether immediately or eventually and bit-by-bit, the dynamic will change. As our half of the equation moves to a better and better place, so will theirs.

In some cases, that may mean that we are happy together, in some cases it means we can at least coexist without harming each other, and in others it means we see that the best path forward is to go on our way in as peaceful a manner as we can to stop any further harm.

Regardless of how things change, our taking responsibility for our own actions and reactions will result in a better situation for us where we are on the path to the Happiness we seek with fewer obstacles and more help – even from those we least expected it from.

Do the Math

- In all situations, the approach remains the same, whether these are one-off or ongoing relationships.

- Start with trying to understand what Happiness each side is seeking, how your Interdependence is playing out due to a misunderstood sense of Happiness, and how changing your actions and reactions will bring out the Impermanent nature of things through acting from a place of understood intentions.

- When relationships are old ones, there may be norms at play that lead us to have expectations of the other person, which in turn may keep us from seeing them as they are currently. The problems in our relationships may actually come from these norms rather than the current definition of Happiness each of us seeks.

V. ADDING UP THE NUMBERS

No matter who we are, and no matter who is around us, we all have relationships that could work better. How much better may differ from one to the next, but there is improvement to be made, and we can all agree that improvement is better than a worsening. You should have tools to begin the improvement process now.

Start with a relationship that matters to you, where improvement is valuable and something you desire, and think about the tools.

Ask yourself what Happiness means for you, and for the other person. Challenge yourself in your answers with whether you are answering truthfully or still reacting. Is your answer what you think it is for them, or what you think they truly feel? You may be able to ask them about their definition of Happiness in some situations, while in others you may not have that luxury. In either case, you need to work toward understanding what the other person truly hopes for. The less it has to do with you, the closer you are to the truth.

After finding potential things they truly care about, you can work on changing the dynamic through the power of Interconnectedness. Think about how the two of you are interacting and feeding the reactions you each have. With your new sense of their Happiness, do you understand better how your actions and reactions could be triggering to them? Keeping that Happiness in mind, would you behave differently? If not, think about your own Happiness, and whether your behavior is leading you closer to that goal or farther away from it. What changes can you make to bring you closer to your Happiness *and* respect their Happiness? With that knowledge in mind, you need to start giving them a different basis to react to.

It is not uncommon to feel hopeless as you go through this exercise. People often seem too stubborn or dug into their position to change. Perhaps that is how you feel about your own position in the relationship. Remember that all things ultimately change through Impermanence. Even if only in small ways, things will evolve. You will each be exposed to different situations in life that will shape your thoughts, and as you change your actions and reactions by focusing on each other's Happiness, you can tap into the power of Impermanence to bring about a shift in the dynamic.

Remember that it does not always happen overnight or instantly. Often, it takes time, and may be something you do for the rest of your relationship. Taking a page from *Do a Day*, you aren't doing this for the rest of your relationship *right now*, so don't worry about that. Be mindful and present in your application of these three core concepts in each interaction you have, and these interactions will add up to a more positive, productive and supportive relationship overall.

It may not always be easy, you may not always do what you should or could, and it may not always be received as you hope it will. But it will make a difference, and that difference will add up over time. Keep at it!

"Radiate boundless love towards the entire world–above, below, and across — unhindered, without ill will, without enmity."

–The Buddha
(from *Metta Sutta*)

VI. ACKNOWLEDGEMENTS

I could never write this book without the relationships around me. Whether that means my own relationships, some of which became examples for this book, or the relationships people I coach shared with me in hopes of making progress themselves. Part of my Happiness comes from appreciating the help others give me, so I want to take a moment to name a few specific people who have done that.

The most crucial place to start is my wife, Sharon, who this book is dedicated to, as is a big chunk of my life. There was a moment in 2004 when I was rendered speechless and stunned as I saw something much greater than just a beautiful woman standing in front of me. I saw a power and a connection that was so clear and so all encompassing, I knew I was looking at someone who would change my life. I couldn't have been more right than I was in that first moment I saw you, Sharon. And change my life did, along with yours, and ours together, several times over. We have been through so much, grown in so many ways, struggled in many moments, and supported each other through it all. I literally would not be the man I am today without you, and for that, I'm thankful. Very thankful.

Another woman who has helped with this book tremendously has no idea she did, and that's Thubten Chodron. You have written literally the most beautiful and inspiring works I've ever read, and they have inspired and impacted me tremendously. Thank you for your mind and how you share it with the world. I hope one day to be able to tell you that in person, but for now, I hope the energy of these words reaches you.

Terah Harrison[8], who wrote the fantastic forward for this book (along with her husband Jeff) gave so much of herself in helping me share the message of *Do a Day*, and work through the applicability and power of *The 50 75 100 Solution* given her knowledge and experience as a counselor working with couples. Terah, you've not only supported me, but made me and my message clearer and stronger. Thank you.

Similarly, Sam and Pat Cullinane, your message (and the great way you two share it) has helped me tremendously as this project came together. Hearing you speak as I was wrapping up the draft of this book, getting to understand your message, and having your support has been invaluable. Your work with Bigger Love[9] and the Not-So Perfect Couple, how you share your honest story of your relationship breaking apart, and how you did the self-work to be able to come back together is so important for all those couples stuck in a way of relating that is pulling them apart.

As I did with *Do a Day*, I also want to thank my editor, Gary Smailes at BubbleCow[10]. I had to work with

---

[8] Learn more about Terah's work and her podcast, *Make More Love Not War*, at http://www.terahharrison.com

[9] Learn more about the Cullinane's work and their books and podcasts at http://www.biggerlove.com

[10] Learn more about Gary's editing services at http://www.bubblecow.com

---

another editor initially, who wasn't really pushing me, and then vanished, missing deadlines and not responding. Gary graciously stepped in at the last minute, turned around an in-depth edit, and helped me move this work to the next level, just as he did with *Do a Day*. Writing this book made it clear to me that his past comments on my work really made me a better writer, which is the most value an editor can bring. Gary, you didn't just edit my work, but helped me edit how I share my thoughts through my writing that made me a better author and communicator overall. For that, I'm thankful.

Lastly, as I did in *Do a Day*, I want to thank you, the reader. And if you were given this book by someone you have a relationship with, thanks to them, too. It can be hard at times to look at ourselves and our contribution to the tougher moments we face, so you deserve recognition for doing that here. I hope you can take the ideas of this book into your relationships right away, thinking about some of the key relationships you have, contemplating the Happiness each of you is seeking and using it to reframe your actions, reactions and the relationship dynamic itself. Finding a way to stand in support of their Happiness rather than seeming to stand in the way of it will serve you well.

I would love to hear from you on how you are building better relationships in your life.

VII. ABOUT THE AUTHOR

Bryan Falchuk is a Certified Personal Trainer and Behavior Change Specialist, who helps people find what really matters to them so they change their lives. He is a professional speaker, life and executive coach, best-selling author, and he is also a father, husband, marathoner, vegan and early-riser.

He had a twenty-year career in Insurance, where he was a C-level executive, and more recently in the technology space helping to grow a startup. Beyond that, professionally, he has devoted himself to helping inspire others to change their lives.

He has presented at multiple TEDx events, had articles published in Inc. Magazine, the *LA Times, Chicago Tribune, Business Insider* and more. He has also been a guest on over 150 podcasts and radio shows, and hosts his own show, The Do a Day Podcast, inspired by his best-selling book, *Do a Day.*

Bryan encourages you to remember, today is a new Day – go out and Do it.

Learn More About Bryan

Bryan Falchuk	www.bryanfalchuk.com
Coaching	www.bryanfalchuk.com/coaching
Speaking	www.bryanfalchuk.com/speaking
Do a Day	www.doadaybook.com
Do a Day Podcast	www.doadaybook.com/podcast

Sign-up To Get Bryan's Latest Updates & News
www.bryanfalchuk.com/signup

Follow Bryan Falchuk on Social Media

Twitter:	@bryanfalchuk
Instagram:	@bryanfalchuk
Facebook:	www.facebook.com/bryanfalchuk
	www.facebook.com/doadaybook
	www.facebook.com/5075100